THE
HUNGARIAN
AMERICANS

THE HUNGARIAN AMERICANS

The Hungarian Experience in North America

Steven Béla Várdy

CHELSEA HOUSE PUBLISHERS

New York   Philadelphia

On the cover: A Hungarian mother and her children at Ellis Island, circa 1905.

CHELSEA HOUSE PUBLISHERS
Editor-in-Chief: Nancy Toff
Executive Editor: Remmel T. Nunn
Managing Editor: Karyn Gullen Browne
Copy Chief: Juliann Barbato
Picture Editor: Adrian G. Allen
Art Director: Maria Epes
Manufacturing Manager: Gerald Levine

The Peoples of North America
Senior Editor: Sean Dolan

Staff for THE HUNGARIAN AMERICANS
Copy Editor: Philip Koslow
Deputy Copy Chief: Nicole Bowen
Editorial Assistant: Elizabeth Nix
Picture Research: PAR/NYC
Assistant Art Director: Loraine Machlin
Senior Designer: Noreen M. Lamb
Production Manager: Joseph Romano
Production Coordinator: Marie Claire Cebrián
Cover Illustration: Paul Biniasz
Banner Design: Hrana L. Janto

First Printing

1 3 5 7 9 8 6 4 2

Library of Congress Cataloging-in-Publication Data
Várdy, Steven Béla, 1935–
    The Hungarian Americans / Steven Béla Várdy.
        p.   cm. -- (Peoples of North America)
    Bibliography: p.
    Includes index.
    Summary: Discusses the history, culture, and religion of the Hungarian Americans;
factors encouraging their emigration; and their acceptance as an ethnic group in North
America.
    ISBN 0-87754-884-6
        0-7910-0292-6 (pbk.)
    1. Hungarian Americans—Juvenile literature. [1. Hungarian
Americans.] I. Title. II. Series.   89-9981
E184.H95V37 1989   CIP
973'.0494511—dc20   AC

CONTENTS

THE PEOPLES OF NORTH AMERICA

CHELSEA HOUSE PUBLISHERS

A NATION
OF NATIONS

Daniel Patrick Moynihan

The Constitution of the United States begins: "We the People of the United States . . ." Yet, as we know, the United States is not made up of a single group of people. It is made up of many peoples. Immigrants from Europe, Asia, Africa, and Central and South America settled in North America seeking a new life filled with opportunities unavailable in their homeland. Coming from many nations, they forged one nation and made it their own. More than 100 years ago, Walt Whitman expressed this perception of America as a melting pot: "Here is not merely a nation, but a teeming Nation of nations."

Although the ingenuity and acts of courage of these immigrants, our ancestors, shaped the North American way of life, we sometimes take their contributions for granted. This fine series, *The Peoples of North America,* examines the experiences and contributions of the immigrants and how these contributions determined the future of the United States and Canada.

Immigrants did not abandon their ethnic traditions when they reached the shores of North America. Each ethnic group had its own customs and traditions, and each brought different experiences, accomplishments, skills, values, styles of dress, and tastes in food that lingered long after its arrival. Yet this profusion of differences created a singularity, or bond, among the immigrants.

The United States and Canada are unusual in this respect. Whereas religious and ethnic differences have sparked intolerance throughout the rest of the world—from the 17th-century religious wars to the 19th-century nationalist movements in Europe to the near extermination of the Jewish people under Nazi Germany—North Americans have struggled to learn how to respect each other's differences and live in harmony.

Millions of immigrants from scores of homelands brought diversity to our continent. In a mass migration, some 12 million immigrants passed through the waiting rooms of New York's Ellis Island; thousands more came to the West Coast. At first, these immigrants were welcomed because labor was needed to meet the demands of the Industrial Age. Soon, however, the new immigrants faced the prejudice of earlier immigrants who saw them as a burden on the economy. Legislation was passed to limit immigration. The Chinese Exclusion Act of 1882 was among the first laws closing the doors to the promise of America. The Japanese were also effectively excluded by this law. In 1924, Congress set immigration quotas on a country-by-country basis.

Such prejudices might have triggered war, as they did in Europe, but North Americans chose negotiation and compromise instead. This determination to resolve differences peacefully has been the hallmark of the peoples of North America.

The remarkable ability of Americans to live together as one people was seriously threatened by the issue of slavery. It was a symptom of growing intolerance in the world. Thousands of settlers from the British Isles had arrived in the colonies as indentured servants, agreeing to work for a specified number of years on farms or as apprentices in return for passage to America and room and board. When the first Africans arrived in the then-British colonies during the 17th century, some colonists thought that they too should be treated as indentured servants. Eventually, the question of whether the Africans should be viewed as indentured, like the English, or as slaves who could be owned for life, was considered in a Maryland court. The court's calamitous decree held that blacks were slaves bound to lifelong servitude, and so were their children. America went through a time of moral examination and civil war before it finally freed African slaves and their descendants. The principle that all people are created equal had faced its greatest challenge and survived.

Yet the court ruling that set blacks apart from other races fanned flames of discrimination that burned long after slavery was abolished—and that still flicker today. The concept of racism had existed for centuries in countries throughout the world. For instance, when the Manchus conquered China in the 13th century, they decreed that Chinese and Manchus could not intermarry. To impress their superiority on the conquered Chinese, the Manchus ordered all Chinese men to wear their hair in a long braid called a queue.

By the 19th century, some intellectuals took up the banner of racism, citing Charles Darwin. Darwin's scientific studies hypothesized that highly evolved animals were dominant over other animals. Some advocates of this theory applied it to humans, asserting that certain races were more highly evolved than others and thus were superior.

This philosophy served as the basis for a new form of discrimination, not only against nonwhite people but also against various ethnic groups. Asians faced harsh discrimination and were depicted by popular 19th-century newspaper cartoonists as depraved, degenerate, and deficient in intelligence. When the Irish flooded American cities to escape the famine in Ireland, the cartoonists caricatured the typical ''Paddy'' (a common term for Irish immigrants) as an apelike creature with jutting jaw and sloping forehead.

By the 20th century, racism and ethnic prejudice had given rise to virulent theories of a Northern European master race. When Adolf Hitler came to power in Germany in 1933, he popularized the notion of Aryan supremacy. *Aryan*, a term referring to the Indo-European races, was applied to so-called superior physical characteristics such as blond hair, blue eyes, and delicate facial features. Anyone with darker and heavier features was considered inferior. Buttressed by these theories, the German Nazi state from

1933 to 1945 set out to destroy European Jews, along with Poles, Russians, and other groups considered inferior. It nearly succeeded. Millions of these people were exterminated.

The tragedies brought on by ethnic and racial intolerance throughout the world demonstrate the importance of North America's efforts to create a society free of prejudice and inequality.

A relatively recent example of the New World's desire to resolve ethnic friction nonviolently is the solution the Canadians found to a conflict between two ethnic groups. A long-standing dispute as to whether Canadian culture was properly English or French resurfaced in the mid-1960s, dividing the peoples of the French-speaking Quebec Province from those of the English-speaking provinces. Relations grew tense, then bitter, then violent. The Royal Commission on Bilingualism and Biculturalism was established to study the growing crisis and to propose measures to ease the tensions. As a result of the commission's recommendations, all official documents and statements from the national government's capital at Ottawa are now issued in both French and English, and bilingual education is encouraged.

The year 1980 marked a coming of age for the United States's ethnic heritage. For the first time, the U.S. Census asked people about their ethnic background. Americans chose from more than 100 groups, including French Basque, Spanish Basque, French Canadian, Afro-American, Peruvian, Armenian, Chinese, and Japanese. The ethnic group with the largest response was English (49.6 million). More than 100 million Americans claimed ancestors from the British Isles, which includes England, Ireland, Wales, and Scotland. There were almost as many Germans (49.2 million) as English. The Irish-American population (40.2 million) was third, but the next largest ethnic group, the Afro-Americans, was a distant fourth (21 million). There was a sizable group of French ancestry (13 million), as well as of Italian (12 million). Poles, Dutch, Swedes, Norwegians, and Russians followed. These groups, and other smaller ones, represent the wondrous profusion of ethnic influences in North America.

Canada, too, has learned more about the diversity of its population. Studies conducted during the French/English conflict showed that Canadians were descended from Ukrainians, Germans, Italians, Chinese, Japanese, native Indians, and Eskimos, among others. Canada found it had no ethnic majority, although nearly half of its immigrant population had come from the British Isles. Canada, like the United States, is a land of immigrants for whom mutual tolerance is a matter of reason as well as principle.

The people of North America are the descendants of one of the greatest migrations in history. And that migration is not over. Koreans, Vietnamese, Nicaraguans, Cubans, and many others are heading for the shores of North America in large numbers. This mix of cultures shapes every aspect of our lives. To understand ourselves, we must know something about our diverse ethnic ancestry. Nothing so defines the North American nations as the motto on the Great Seal of the United States: *E Pluribus Unum*— Out of Many, One.

BEYOND THE NUMBERS

Since the first Hungarian immigrant stepped upon the shores of the North American continent in the 16th century, about 900,000 of his countrymen have followed and made the United States or Canada their permanent home. About 88 percent of those, or some 800,000 Hungarians, settled in the United States. The majority—650,000—arrived in the United States between 1870 and 1914, during the great wave of immigration from eastern and southern Europe, with the greatest number of those arriving during the first decade of the 20th century. More than half—60,000—of the Hungarians who immigrated to Canada did so in the decades following World War II, with the high point occurring in the 1950s.

According to the 1980 census, nearly 1.8 million American citizens claim to be of Hungarian origin. About 727,000 of them are immigrants or their immediate descendants and are still fully Hungarian. The rest are the products of mixed marriages but consider themselves to be Hungarian Americans. Approximately 116,000 Hungarian immigrants and their direct descendants live in Canada, where an additional 28,000 claim some degree of Hungarian ancestry. Together, this adds up to about 2 million North Americans with Hungarian roots, a quite sizable group whose presence has greatly influenced, in ways that later chapters will explore, both U.S. and Canadian society.

Hungarians in the U.S.	
New York	245,000
Ohio	243,000
Pennsylvania	203,000
New Jersey	168,000
California	165,000
Michigan	127,000
Florida	90,000
Illinois	85,000
Connecticut	53,000
Indiana	44,000
Wisconsin	33,000
Maryland	28,000
Texas	28,000
Virginia	22,000
Massachusetts	20,000
Arizona	19,000
Colorado	16,000
Washington	16,000
Oregon	11,000
Georgia	10,000
North Carolina	9,000

Hungarian-American population by state, according to the 1980 U.S. census.

Before and immediately after World War I, the great majority of Hungarian immigrants and their descendants settled in about a dozen northeastern states, mostly in the region between New York City and Chicago. In 1920, for example, New York, Ohio, Pennsylvania, New Jersey, Illinois, Michigan, Connecticut, Indiana, Wisconsin, Missouri, and West Virginia were home to sizable Hungarian-American populations. As of that year, only 5,200 lived in California, whereas the rest were widely dispersed throughout dozens of other states.

By 1980 the situation had changed dramatically. Although the majority of Hungarian Americans still lived in the Northeast, a significant number of them had moved to the Pacific Coast, the Southwest, and the South, as seen in the accompanying chart. Significant demographic changes also occurred in Canada. In 1921 three-fourths of Canada's 13,000 Hungarians lived in rural settlements in the western provinces of Saskatchewan, Alberta, and Manitoba, 9,000 in Saskatchewan alone. By 1981 more than four-fifths of the country's 144,000 Hungarians were city dwellers. Seventy-three thousand, or just over half, lived in the Province of Ontario, in such cities as Toronto, Hamilton, Saint Catharines, Welland, Niagara Falls, Ottawa, and Windsor. The rest were concentrated in Montreal, in the Province of Quebec; in Vancouver, British Columbia; and in Calgary and Edmonton in Alberta. Saskatchewan's share of the Hungarian population had declined to less than 10 percent.

Valued Contributors

Their numbers alone do not make the Hungarian Americans a unique ethnic group. In the United States, they are outnumbered by many other groups, including the English, the Scots, the Poles, the Germans, the Irish, and others, but more than numbers are needed to assess the significance of a people. And in terms of contributions to their adopted society, the Hungarian Americans are second to none. Indeed, it may be argued that since the period between the two world wars, Hungarian Americans have played a decisive role in shaping American and Canadian culture and

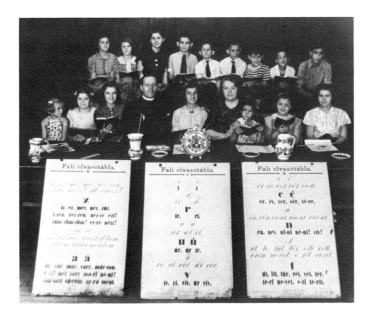

Hungarian-American children study with the aid of Hungarian-language charts. Hungarian, spoken by 13 million people, is related to the Finnish and Estonian languages.

civilization. This is particularly true in the areas of atomic science, mathematics and computers, music and the arts, the film industry, and, more recently, business and philanthropy.

The Hungarian Impact on America

The large majority of Hungarians who immigrated to the United States and Canada between 1870 and 1914 were peasants or unskilled workers, mostly from the rural regions of north, east, and northeast Hungary. Unable to find jobs or provide satisfactorily for their family in the homeland, these economic immigrants came to the New World in search of work. This first generation provided the sinew and sweat that helped America transform itself into an industrial power in the period between the Civil War and World War I. Later, a different type of immigrant began to arrive. Between the two world wars, increasing numbers of artisans, skilled workers, professionals, and intellectuals felt compelled by economic conditions or their political beliefs to leave Hungary. Yet it was not until after World War II that the United States and Canada felt the full impact of the immigration of the educated middle and upper layers of Hungarian society. In the United

States, this influx resulted in a change in the leadership of the immigrant community, which as a result wielded greater political and cultural influence. In Canada, the postwar newcomers helped transform the Hungarian immigrant community from a numerically small group located in isolated rural enclaves to a sizable, urban-based entity. If it may be said that the first generation of Hungarian immigrants contributed its brawn, then this new generation offered its brains, leading to a number of scientific breakthroughs and cultural developments that had a significant impact not only on America but also on the world.

Perhaps the most visible example of the impact was the role played by Hungarian immigrants in the development of the United States's atomic power during the 1940s. The most important such work was done in conjunction with the Manhattan Project, as the top secret project to develop the atom bomb was called. As Laura Fermi has noted in her book *Illustrious Immigrants: The Intellectual Migration from Europe 1930-1941*, the "scientific brain power" used to develop the weapon that made the United States the preeminent power of the day "was furnished by three Hungarians [Leo Szilárd, Eugene Wigner, and Edward Teller] and one Italian [Enrico Fermi]." Hungarian immigrants also contributed to the birth of America's computer age (John von Neumann); to the development of jet power and aerodynamics in general (Theodor von Kármán); to the rise of the American film industry (Adolph Zukor, William Fox, George Cukor); and to the growing appreciation of classical music in this country (Eugene Ormandy, George Széll, Sir George Solti, and others). During various periods from the 1950s to the 1980s, seven Hungarian or Hungarian-American Nobel laureates and many other scientists and academics of similar caliber were employed at American universities and research institutes. One can hardly move in the middle and upper layers of American and Canadian scientific, artistic, scholarly, and financial circles without encountering Hungarians or persons of Hungarian extraction.

Naturally, not all Hungarian immigrants and their descendants were or are top scientists, scholars, or artists. Most of them are everyday citizens employed in diverse occupations, from skilled workers through the various professions. Be they native born or newcomers, professional or laborer, most Hungarians have inherited or brought with them a belief in solid family life, a powerful work ethic, and the drive to succeed.

Although many Hungarians faced the usual difficulties in forging a new life in the New World—poverty, language barriers, prejudice—most believe that the United States and Canada have generally been good to them and their compatriots, a generosity that they reciprocate by contributing their drive, inventiveness, and creativity to their new homelands. In recent years, some of those Hungarian Americans who have been fortunate enough to achieve a high level of economic success have been celebrated for their largesse in giving something back to the community. Perhaps the best-publicized example is the philanthropic activities of the American-born entrepreneur Eugene M. Lang, who initiated the "I Have a Dream" program in New York City, which pledges payment of college tuition for youths at a Harlem grade school who stay in school and maintain a certain level of academic achievement.

A Political People

One area in which Hungarian Americans have not achieved a conspicuous level of achievement is politics. They do not maintain a significant Hungarian lobby in either Washington, D.C., or Ottawa, Ontario, and few members of the U.S. Congress have boasted Hungarian ancestry. But one should not conclude from this that Hungarian Americans are politically apathetic. Although they have been slow to involve themselves in American politics, many Hungarian Americans have been or are intensely interested in political issues. The primary reason for this hesitance is their "Hungarocentrism," or tendency to look at events from the viewpoint of Hungary, even after settling in North America. Because so many of the early economic immigrants came to the New World with the intention of staying only temporarily, few took an intense interest in the politics of the United States. Those who nurtured the dream of returning to the homeland

The members of the Polgar family were among the last of nearly 30,000 Hungarians to leave the refugee reception center at Camp Kilmer, New Jersey, in May 1957. The Hungarian words on the sign over the gate mean "God has brought you to America."

saw no reason to bother with obtaining U.S. citizenship, the necessary first step toward political involvement. Many were unlettered and unfamiliar with democratic processes, conditions that kept them from political participation.

By contrast, the political immigrants of the postwar period brought with them a history of political activism. Most had been driven to emigrate because of their opposition to the Communist government that the Soviet Union had helped install in Hungary in 1948, but their involvement in the struggle against communism and their desire to return to a liberated Hungary left them with little time or desire to concentrate on domestic American or Canadian political issues. It was only during the 1970s, with the rise of the first post–World War II American-born or American-educated generation, that this attitude began to change.

Despite the continued Hungarocentrism of the immigrants, their relationship to the old country has often been a complicated one. Before World War II, the Hungarian government tried to use the real or imagined influence of the immigrants to further its own political and economic goals, but because so many of the political immigrants opposed Hungary's wartime alliance with Nazi Germany and the postwar Communist regime, in recent years Hungarian Americans have often found themselves in an adversary relationship with the government of their homeland.

This situation began to change somewhat in the 1960s when the Hungarian government introduced liberalization measures that eased travel restrictions and made it possible for immigrants to visit the homeland, but this gesture of reconciliation created divisions within the immigrant community. Some wished to forget, or at least forgive, past differences and resume their relationship with the old country. Others remained adamant about maintaining their struggle against the Communist government until Hungary is "liberated." Although more than two decades have passed since the beginnings of Hungary's liberalization, these two camps have still been unable to solve their differences. A resolution may not be possible until the native-born children of the postwar immigrant generation, who presumably have less of an emotional stake in the politics of the homeland, rise to positions of leadership within the immigrant community, although these differences may disappear if the liberalization measures (a market economy, freedom of movement, etc.) introduced in Hungary at the end of the 1980s prove to be harbingers of permanent change.

A Hungarian-American youth studies in a special Hungarian-language class at the Saint Ladislaus school in New Brunswick, New Jersey.

Maintaining an Identity

At present, the greatest problem faced by the Hungarians of North America is to what extent they will survive as a distinct ethnic group. Being very much a part of the fast-paced, largely urban societies of the United States and Canada, they are eager to attain success on American terms. Unlike their forerunners, the economic immigrants who were forced by prejudice, poverty, and fear to live in the ethnic ghettos known as Little Hungaries, today's Hungarian Americans see no need to limit themselves to the narrow confines of such ethnic enclaves. Their determination to avail themselves of all that their new countries have to offer has brought them much reward, but it has also created conflict over how much of their Hungarian identity should and can be maintained. What constitutes this Hungarian identity, and the story of how Hungarians have struggled to define themselves in the context of their adopted societies, is the subject of the rest of this book.

Hungary's most important national symbol, the Holy Crown of Saint Stephen, which was brought to the United States after U.S. soldiers discovered it in a Hungarian salt mine in 1945. The crown was returned to the Hungarian government amid much controversy in 1978 and is now displayed in the National Museum in Budapest.

HUNGARY AND
THE HUNGARIANS

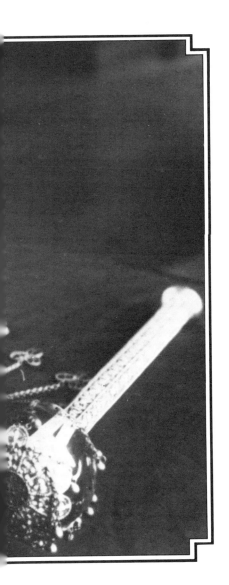

Hungary sits squarely in the middle of east-central Europe, bordered by Austria to the west, Czechoslovakia and the Soviet Union to the north, Romania to the east, and Yugoslavia to the south. Bisected by the Danube River, the Hungarian landscape includes vineyards, rolling hills, and fields of lavender, but for all the nation's beauty and diversity, some of its people consider it incomplete. Late-20th-century Hungary differs in many ways from the nation that in 1914 stood among the world powers of the day. After World War I, Hungary was made to forfeit two-thirds of the territory it had claimed as its own. Whereas Hungary once controlled vast expanses of land throughout central Europe, it now lays claim to a mere 36,000 square miles, which makes it approximately the size of Indiana. A decrease in population accompanied this physical reduction, from about 22 million in 1914 to 10.6 million in the 1980s, and Hungary's power in world politics has waned as well. After World War II, the republic fell under the control of the Soviet Union, with which it remains closely tied. Although Hungary enjoys some degree of autonomy, it still must comply with international and domestic policies dictated by the Soviet Union. To the proud Hungarians, the reduced circumstances of the nation's present stand in sharp contrast to its often glorious past.

Modern Hungary. The nation once controlled lands that now belong to Czechoslovakia, Romania, and Yugoslavia.

The Magyars

The ancestors of today's Hungarians, the Magyars, originally lived in the western corner of what is now the Soviet Union. There, over time, they intermingled with Turkic tribes that had migrated west from Central Asia. Although they retained their unique language, which belongs to the linguistic family called Finno-Urgic and is unrelated to any of the European languages, these early Hungarian tribesmen adopted many other aspects of Turkic culture. The name *Magyar*, in fact, is derived from the Turkic word *onogur*, meaning "ten tribes."

The Hungarians lived among the Turks for nearly 1,000 years, all the time gradually moving southward and westward until they occupied the area surrounding the Danube River in the region that is modern Hungary. By A.D. 896 the 10 (although Hungarians traditionally speak of 7 tribes) Hungarian tribes had united under the leadership of Arpád, the head of the most powerful Hungarian tribe. Under Arpád's leadership the Hungarians fought off their rivals for this territory, such as the neighboring Moravians, and began absorbing other ethnic groups of the Danube region into their society. Soon afterward, Hungary's pagan rulers began looking to expand their influence. Magyar warriors swept into Germany, France, and Italy and soon developed a reputation for horsemanship, fighting prowess, and ruthlessness.

Christian Europe's fear of the ferocious, pagan Magyars eased somewhat after 955, when the German king Otto the Great soundly defeated them at the Battle of Lech. With Hungary also under pressure on its eastern borders, Géza, Arpád's great-grandson, determined to make peace with western Europe. The cornerstone of his policy was to be the introduction of Christianity to the Hungarians, and in 973 he asked the Holy Roman Emperor Otto II to dispatch missionaries to convert his countrymen.

Although Géza died before seeing the successful Christianization of his people, his son and successor, Stephen, carried on his work so zealously that he was later canonized by the Catholic church. Christianization had profound consequences for Hungary. Stephen was crowned king of Hungary by the pope in the year 1000 and was granted the power to administer the church within Hungary autonomously, which gave him enormous political as well as religious authority. This concentration of power in the person of the king helped bring about the creation of a centralized government and the formation of a modern political state. Its conversion also allowed Hungary to take its place among the other Christian nations of Europe and helped ensure its independence, for it is unlikely that the great European powers would long have tolerated a nation of infidels in their midst, no matter how fierce swordsmen or adept horsemen its people were. By adapting Christianity, Hungary also tapped into the single most important unifying element of European culture at the time.

Stephen did more than just convert Hungary to Christianity. He founded a powerful and enduring monarchy; built churches, monasteries, and schools;

Hungarian stamp showing Stephen, Hungary's first king, and Queen Gisella. Stephen received the legendary crown from Pope Sylvester II, and during his long reign (1000–1038) the Magyar nation was consolidated and Christianized. Canonized in 1083, Saint Stephen is Hungary's greatest national hero.

fortified castles, and walled cities, and protected Hungary from invasion. Stephen also established a centralized royal administration and tax-collection system and introduced advanced methods of agriculture, manufacturing, and commerce. Hungarians credit him with transforming Hungary into a modern state, and he remains the most revered figure in their history.

Stephen's groundwork enabled Hungary to preserve its independence into the 16th century despite the constant threat of invasion posed by its belligerent neighbors, the German-led Holy Roman Empire to the west and the Ottoman Empire of the Turks to the east. Succeeding kings proved less capable, although Mátyás, who reigned from 1485 to 1490, presided over a flowering of Hungarian culture and military successes that led to his brief kingship's characterization as a golden age. But having overrun most of the Middle East and a good part of the Balkan peninsula, by the 1520s the Ottoman Turks, under the leadership of Sultan Süleyman the Magnificent, were poised to move on eastern and central Europe. In August 1526, at the Battle of Mohács, Süleyman's legions routed 20,000 Hungarian troops commanded by King Louis II. Louis

The artillery of Süleyman the Magnificent at the siege of the Hungarian town of Szigetvár in 1524. Despite Hungary's defeat, resistance to the Turks became the stuff of popular legend.

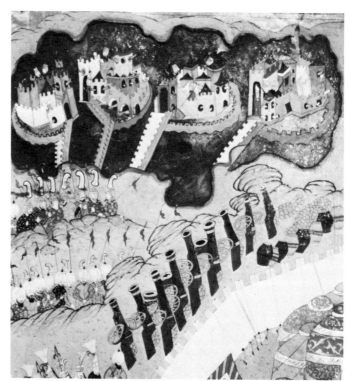

and many of the country's most important nobles were killed in the fighting.

In the wake of the defeat, Hungary's ruling families fought among themselves over who should succeed Louis and failed to unite in opposition to the Ottoman invaders. By 1541, Süleyman had seized the city of Buda and most of the central part of Hungary. North and west Hungary were controlled by the Hapsburg emperor Ferdinand I, while Isabella, the widow of János Zápolya, Mátyás's great-grandson, governed the eastern region known as Transylvania. Although the Ottomans largely dictated Transylvania's foreign policy, its nominal independence proved crucial to the preservation of a Hungarian national identity, and Hungarian culture thrived there during the 150 years of Ottoman domination.

Under the Hapsburgs

As the Ottoman Empire weakened because of internal dissension and corruption, its Hungarian lands were gradually wrested from it by the Hapsburg Empire, whose capital was the Austrian city of Vienna. In 1686, Hapsburg armies reclaimed Buda from Turkish forces and set out to liberate all of Hungary. Thirteen years later, by virtue of the Treaty of Karlowitz, the Turks relinquished their Hungarian holdings to the Hapsburgs, but the Magyars and their descendants were no more pleased at having to pledge fealty to an Austrian imperial overlord than they had been with swearing loyalty to the Turkish sultan. Led by Prince Ferenc Rákóczi II, the Hungarians rose up to throw off the Hapsburgs. The Rákóczi War of Liberation ended in 1711 with the Peace of Szatmár, which mandated that although Hungary would remain a part of the Hapsburg Empire, for the most part it would function autonomously, under its own laws, government, and administrative system.

This political status quo was maintained for some time, although the Hungarians remained restive under Hapsburg rule. The peasantry resented the excessive taxation and land seizures that kept it in poverty, and patriotic Hungarians chafed at being tied to a foreign dynasty. Virtually the entire populace was angered by

Prince Ferenc Rákóczi II of Transylvania returned from exile in 1703 to lead Hungarian insurrectionist forces against the Hapsburgs.

Liberty Square in Budapest. The Parliament House, in the background, is one of the world's largest legislative buildings.

Hapsburg decrees that made German the compulsory language for all government and official business. Most upsetting of all was the Hapsburg policy of resettling Germans and South Slavic peoples in Hungary. The Turkish and Austrian wars had already reduced Hungary's population by nearly 40 percent between 1500 and 1720; the Hapsburg policy of plantation reduced Hungarians to about 45 percent of the population of their own country.

Hungarian nationalism, which was born among the Royal Hungarian Guard regiments in Vienna in the 1770s, began to flourish in the 1820s. It centered on the struggle by intellectuals and nobles to replace German, the language of government, and Latin, since Saint Stephen's day the language of learning and culture, with Hungarian. Pride in Hungary's language and culture went hand in hand with demands for political reform and increased independence and in the 1840s drew inspiration from similar movements then arising throughout Europe. Led by Lajos Kossuth, a landless noble and relentless agitator for change, and the revolutionary poet Sándor Petőfi, the reform movement grew in strength until 1848, when revolutions aimed against many of the European monarchies broke out. In Hungary, Petőfi and like-minded writers took to the streets in the city of Pest, and liberal members of the Diet, or national assembly, enacted legislation, known as the March laws, that greatly reduced the Hapsburg monarch's power, provided for greatly increased political participation by the people, liberated the peasantry from excessive taxation and other restrictions, and allowed complete freedom of the press and religion.

Not surprisingly, the Hapsburg government did not welcome the changes. They first encouraged rebellion by the many national minorities within Hungary, notably the Croatians, a South Slavic people whose homeland is now part of Yugoslavia but was then governed by Hungary, and the Romanians, who had slowly become a majority in Transylvania. When the Hungarian home defense force defeated the Croats and Kossuth declared his nation's independence, Hapsburg troops moved on Hungary. Initially rebuffed, they were ultimately successful, restoring Hapsburg rule and thus setting in motion the first significant wave of Hungarian immigration. Kossuth, who had been named president of the short-lived independent state of Hungary, was among those who fled. He spent some time in the United States, where he was successful in creating pro-Hungary sympathy.

Hungarian unrest continued, and in 1867 the Hapsburg government and the moderate faction in the Hungarian Diet, led by Ferenc Deák, reached a compromise, known as the Austro-Hungarian Compromise (Ausgleich in German), which established the Dual Monarchy. Under its terms the two countries maintained their own constitutions, ministries, and parliaments and exercised complete control over their internal affairs. Citizenship was also controlled by each country individually. Austria and Hungary shared ministers of defense, finance, and foreign relations; the Hapsburg monarch was both emperor of Austria and king of Hungary. Each nation controlled its own fi-

Lajos Kossuth (1802–94), leader of the mid-19th-century Hungarian nationalist revival, proclaimed a short-lived independent Hungarian republic in 1848. He became the symbol of Hungarian nationalism.

nances, but the dual minister of finance oversaw the budget for foreign affairs and the military. The Dual Monarchy remained in place until Austria-Hungary's defeat in World War I, and it was from this singular state that the economic immigrants who constituted the first great wave of Hungarian immigration came.

Dualist Hungary

During Austria-Hungary's five decades, Hungary underwent great economic, cultural, and political development, as manifested by increased industrialization and urbanization and a rise in scholarship and scientific and cultural achievement. Hungary's single greatest period of economic expansion occurred during the era of the Dual Monarchy. The country's railroad, milling, and banking industries grew, as did foreign and domestic trade. Although Hungary would never reach the same level of industrial development as Austria, its economy enjoyed a faster rate of growth during this time. Emblematic of Hungary's transformation during the period was the merger of the modest medieval towns of Buda and Pest—each resting on opposite sides of the Danube River—to form the modern capital city of Budapest. Formally united in 1873, Budapest soon grew into a thriving metropolis, a political, cultural, and economic center that rivaled the imperial capital at Vienna.

The age of the Austro-Hungarian Empire also witnessed a new commitment to education and literacy in Hungary. After the passage of the Universal Education Act of 1868, general school attendance improved dramatically, with 90 percent of school-age children attending class on a regular basis. The expansion of elementary education was paralleled by similar developments in secondary and higher education. By the turn of the century, the formerly provincial University of Budapest took its place among the ranks of noted European educational institutions. At about the same time, such specialized and soon-to-be-renowned institutions of higher learning as the College of Fine Arts and the Conservatory of Music were established in Budapest (the latter founded by the famed pianist and composer Franz Liszt), as well as a series of professional schools, libraries, museums, and theaters. Combined with a general spirit of economic and political liberalism, these institutions gave birth to the first generation of secular Hungarian intellectuals, figures such as Liszt, the poet János Arany, and the novelist Mór Jókai, whose achievements made Budapest one of the most cosmopolitan capitals in Europe.

For the peasantry, however, life during the dualist period was not as pleasant. Although freed of their obligations to the nobility, they were without true political representation and were seldom able to take advantage of advanced educational opportunities, which remained the almost exclusive province of the upper classes. Even worse, most were unable to amass enough land to farm profitably because land ownership remained concentrated in the hands of the

During the Dual Monarchy (1867–1919) many Hungarian peasants, such as these farmers, immigrated to North America in search of better opportunities.

wealthy. As their economic and political situation worsened, many decided to leave Hungary and seek their fortune in North America.

Hungary After the Wars

World War I, which lasted from 1914 to 1918, resulted in drastic changes for Hungary, which fought with the losing Central Powers (Germany, Austria, and the tottering Ottoman Empire) against the Allies (France, Great Britain, Russia, and the United States). By virtue of the Treaty of Trianon, one of the many postwar agreements that rearranged the political and geographic face of Europe, Hungary was compelled by the victors to relinquish more than 70 percent of its land, which was home to nearly 65 percent of its population. Most of this territory was given to the newly created states of Czechoslovakia, Romania, and the Kingdom of the Serbs, Croats, and Slovenes, later known as Yugoslavia.

New political leadership arose to take charge in postwar Hungary. Just after the war ended, Béla Kun, a Hungarian prisoner of war, returned to Budapest

Admiral Miklós Horthy, the last commander in chief of the Austro-Hungarian navy, is welcomed as the newly chosen regent of Hungary in November 1919 by the residents of Budapest. Horthy's regime encouraged nationalism, but it failed to provide many of the political, social, and economic reforms that Hungary needed.

from Russia, where he had been greatly impressed by the Russian Communists. Led by Vladimir Lenin, the Russian Communists, known as the Bolsheviks, had helped overthrow the Russian monarchy and had established their own government. Once home, Kun organized a Hungarian Communist party, which took over the government in March 1919. Kun's regime lasted only eight months before being toppled in a coup by a group of former Hapsburg military officers, led by Admiral Miklós Horthy. In November 1919, Horthy restored the Hungarian monarchy and instated himself as the country's regent, inaugurating a controlled parliamentary system, criticized by some as a dictatorship, that lasted until the outbreak of World War II.

Hungary's early flirtation with communism had important consequences for its foreign policy. In the 1930s, as much of Europe became an ideological battleground between the opposing political creeds of fascism, as practiced by the dictators Benito Mussolini in Italy, Adolf Hitler in Germany, and Francisco Franco in Spain, and communism, as practiced in the Soviet Union under the dictatorship of Josef Stalin, Hungary trod a fine line between the two, a tightrope act that became more perilous once Germany annexed Austria

These Hungarian soldiers were among the 20,000 who surrendered to the Soviet army during fighting in the Carpathian Mountains in November 1944. The soldiers claimed that they no longer wanted to fight for Hitler or his hopeless cause.

Freedom fighters take aim against Soviet forces in Budapest in November 1956. Despite fierce resistance, the Soviets quelled the revolution in a few weeks. Thousands of Hungarians were killed or imprisoned, and more than 200,000 fled the country.

in 1938. Gradually, Hungary's fear of the Soviet Union moved it toward a policy of limited cooperation with Nazi Germany, which also promised Hungary restoration of the lands taken from it following World War I. Once World War II began, friendship with Germany enabled Horthy to reclaim former Hungarian lands in Yugoslavia and Romania, and ultimately Hungary declared war on the Soviet Union.

There was also a good deal of pro-Allied sentiment in Hungary (the Allies—France, Great Britain, the United States, and the Soviet Union—fought against Germany and Japan in World War II), which enabled Hungary for a time to protect its Jewish population against the policy of extermination imposed by Hitler. But this pro-Allied sentiment led to Hitler's occupying Hungary in March 1944, and the Germans soon began deporting Hungary's Jews, despite the opposition of

Horthy and Hungary's resistance movement. In late 1944, Soviet troops invaded Hungary and began fighting their way toward Budapest, which fell on February 13, 1945, two months before Germany's surrender. During the last year of the war about 1 million Hungarians were permanently dislocated.

After the war ended, the Soviets remained an important influence in Hungary, which became a republic in February 1946, with Zoltán Tildy as its elected president. Two years later a Soviet-backed coup d'etat forced Tildy from office, and a Communist government, answerable directly to Moscow, was installed. The Soviet influence was evident in virtually every facet of Hungarian life. Farms were collectivized on the Soviet model, dissidents were sentenced to terms of forced labor following "show trials" much like those that had terrorized Moscow's intellectual community in the 1930s, and Hungarian schoolchildren were subjected to a program of "Russification" in which they were forcibly taught the Russian language and Russian customs.

This period of intense authoritarianism came to an end in October 1956 when student demonstrators in Budapest, demanding independence and free elections, were fired upon by police. A nationwide uprising ensued and was put down only after savage fighting between the Hungarians and the invading Soviet forces. Although the Soviets crushed the revolt, installed János Kádár as premier, and stationed more than 50,000 troops in Hungary, it proved impossible to fully restore the old system. After an initial period of repression and retribution, Kádár began to liberalize Hungary's economic, political, and cultural life. In 1968 the government introduced the New Economic Mechanism (NEM), a program that moved Hungary away from traditional Communist economic models toward a hybrid of capitalist and Communist economic policies known popularly as "goulash communism." By the 1970s, Hungary's economic and political liberalization had progressed to the point where the country was the envy of its Warsaw Pact neighbors. (The Warsaw Pact is the mutual defense treaty that unites the Communist nations of Eastern Europe.) Individual wealth increased, and the Hungarians felt increasingly

János Kádár, installed as premier by the Soviets, delivers a speech to the first session of the Hungarian Parliament following the 1956 revolution. After an initial period of fierce repression, the Kádár regime instituted some measures of economic liberalization.

Farmers debate a new collective-farm project in 1959. The cooperative included 63 families and about 1,500 acres of land. After years of resistance to farm collectivization, Hungary's peasants began joining cooperatives in the late 1950s, and by 1962 more than 96 percent of Hungary's farmland was collectivized.

free to criticize openly their leaders and their system of government. They were also able to travel much more freely than their counterparts in the Soviet bloc.

These developments were not achieved without a price. The gap between the wealthy and the poor in Hungarian society grew more pronounced, and the country became progressively indebted to the West. By 1988, Hungary's per capita debt was the highest among the East European states, and its total indebtedness had surpassed $18 billion. Its leaders felt they had no choice but to institute austerity measures, such as taxing cigarettes, liquor, and other luxury products, but these belt-tightening policies dissatisfied many

Hungarians. An extremely vocal dissident movement arose in protest.

In May 1988, Kádár was replaced by the younger and apparently more flexible and pragmatic Károly Grósz. Under his leadership Hungary became the first of the Soviet bloc states to introduce a Western-style income tax. The government also granted all citizens the right to leave the country if they could afford to do so financially. Next, it passed a law that made it possible for individuals who do not belong to the Communist party to run for elected office, including seats in the Hungarian Parliament. In the spring of 1989 a multiparty system was introduced. By allowing a ceremonial reburial of the leaders of the 1956 revolution, including Imre Nagy, in June of that year, the government attempted to assuage much of the bitterness that remained from that bloody time. (Following his execution by hanging, Nagy had been buried in an unmarked grave. Even his widow was denied knowledge of where his remains rested.) While these and similar reforms did not completely alleviate Hungary's growing economic crisis, they made the country into the most flexible and progressive of the East European states.

Border guards begin dismantling fortifications on the Austrian frontier in May 1989 as Hungary becomes the first country in the Soviet bloc to lift the Iron Curtain that has separated Eastern Europe from the West since World War II.

SZABADSÁG LIBERTY

1-2   1-8

HUSZONHARMADIK ÉVFOLYAM   1913. JANUÁR 4   TWENTYTHIRD YEAR   MAGAZINE

KI MEGELŐZTE COLUMBUST

FROM FORTY-NINERS TO FIFTY-SIXERS

Hungarian travelers and adventurers have been coming to North America ever since the late 16th century, but it was not until after the revolution of 1848 and the creation of Austria-Hungary in 1867 that a significant number of Hungarian citizens left their native land for North America. By World War I, this mass migration had brought about 4 million "Austro-Hungarians"—among them 1.7 million Hungarian citizens and close to 650,000 ethnic Hungarians or Magyars—to the United States and Canada.

Many of these early immigrants liked to recount the story of the first Hungarian known to have set foot on American soil, Stephen Parmenius of Buda, known as "the learned" because of his scholarly talents. Born in 1555, Parmenius left Hungary in 1579 to continue his studies, first at the University of Heidelberg in Germany and then at Oxford University in England. In 1583 he was asked by the explorer Sir Humphrey Gilbert to join his expedition to North America, where—according to Queen Elizabeth's royal charter—Gilbert was "to discover, occupy, and to possess heathen lands not actually possessed of any Christian prince or people." Little did Parmenius realize that this expedi-

Sándor Bölöni-Farkas wrote Journey to North America *as a record of his travels in America in 1831. His book convinced many Hungarians to immigrate to North America.*

tion to the New World would be his last as well as his first. He drowned only three weeks after his arrival, on August 29, 1583, in a shipwreck off Sable Island near the coast of Nova Scotia.

In the period between Parmenius's death and the arrival of the first wave of immigrants—political exiles from the revolution of 1848—the Hungarians were represented in North America by Jesuit missionaries, Protestant dissenters, and a handful of explorers. Driven by wanderlust, religious zeal, or the desire to practice freely the creed of their choice, these early arrivals did not have a great overall impact on American society, although some made important individual contributions. One such person is Colonel Michael Kováts, who is generally credited with having been the founder of the American cavalry. Kováts joined the cause of American independence in the spring of 1777, when he was 53, serving as the "master of exercise" of the famed Pulaski legion, led by the Polish soldier Casimir Pulaski. After Kováts's death in May 1779 at the Battle of Charleston, his feats as a military leader were praised by one of his opponents, the British major F. Skelly, who recorded in his *Journal of a Brigade Major* that Kováts was "the rebels' most able soldier."

Hungarian travelers—that is, those who visited the United States and Canada without necessarily intending to stay—played an important role in the history of Hungarian immigration to North America. Perhaps the most notable of these visitors were Sándor Bölöni-Farkas (1790–1842) and Ágoston Haraszthy (1812–69). Bölöni-Farkas visited America in 1831 and was both charmed and overawed by what he found. His *Journey to North America*, written after his return to Hungary and published in 1834, contains his impressions of the United States, which he characterizes as a "happy country" that is there to serve both as a "stern warning to the despots as well as an inspiring beacon to the oppressed." His words stuck in the mind of his Hungarian contemporaries and helped direct millions of them to North America when they left their native land.

A decade after Bölöni-Farkas's work was published, Ágoston Haraszthy wrote an almost equally influential book about his experiences in the United

States. After the publication of his *Journey to North America* in 1844, he decided to leave his native country altogether and return to America as a permanent settler, with his wife, children, and elderly parents in tow. After a brief stint in Wisconsin, he moved on to California, where he introduced European grapes to California's Sonoma Valley and also wrote the first American handbook on viticulture, *Grape Culture, Wines, and Wine-Making*. For his contributions, Haraszthy is rightfully considered to be the father of California's wine industry.

For Freedom

Ágoston Haraszthy was at once the last noted Hungarian adventurer and the first notable Hungarian immigrant to the United States. His decision to settle in America took place only a few years before the first large Hungarian immigration to North America, which followed the defeat of the Hungarian revolution of 1848–49. The Hungarian uprising incited strong retribution on the part of the Viennese imperial authorities, and the harsh policies imposed by Hungary's Austrian rulers triggered a mass flight by patriotic Hungarians.

As many as 4,000 of these political refugees eventually journeyed to North America. Among them was Lajos Kossuth, the leader of the revolution, who for a brief period created a virtual "Kossuth-craze" in Amer-

A bond issued in the United States following the failed Hungarian revolution of 1848. To escape Austrian reprisal, many Hungarian patriots fled to North America, where they continued the struggle for an independent Hungarian government. The bond was sold to raise funds for the independence movement.

Major General Julius H. Stahel (1825–1912) was just one of many Hungarian Americans who fought to preserve the Union during the American Civil War. Although wounded, Stahel led a cavalry charge that decided the Battle of Piedmont, Virginia, in favor of the Union army. He received the Congressional Medal of Honor for his bravery.

ica. But as Kossuth wished to continue the struggle agaianst Austria, he stayed for only seven months. Very few of the "forty-niners," as they were known, came with the intention of staying, but ultimately most of them remained. Those who eventually decided to return to Hungary did so only after the Compromise of 1867, the agreement that created the Dual Monarchy. Most of the forty-niners were people of learning, such as John Xantus, an explorer and naturalist who documented the flora and fauna of the American West and Baja California; Alexander Asbóths, an engineer, who helped plan New York City's Central Park; and Michael Heilperin, an editor of Appleton's *New American Encyclopaedia*, who won a place amid the reigning American intellectuals of his day.

Patriots in the old country, the forty-niners distinguished themselves as soldiers in their new homeland. Of the 4,000 Hungarians then in the United States, about 900 served in the American Civil War. More than a hundred of this number were officers in the Union army. One of the seven Hungarian generals to serve, Major General Julius H. Stahel, was also the first Hungarian recipient of the Congressional Medal of Honor. Few of his contemporaries knew that this famed Hungarian-American military leader—who stood at Abraham Lincoln's side when the president delivered the Gettysburg Address—began his adult life as a humble bookstore clerk in Hungary under the name of Gyula Számvald.

The Great Economic Immigration

The 50 years between the Civil War and the First World War was the period of the greatest mass migration in world history. During this time more than 20 million Europeans crossed the Atlantic to North America. Approximately 1.7 million Hungarian citizens emigrated to the United States, and another 8,000 Hungarians went to Canada.

A different type of immigrant made up this new wave. Most of the Hungarian immigrants of the late 19th and early 20th centuries were neither adventurers, missionaries, travelers, nor political refugees but

economic immigrants who wanted to escape the hardships of their native land. They planned to make their fortunes in America and then return to Hungary, where they hoped to create a better and more satisfying life for themselves and their families. Ultimately most of them stayed.

The vast majority of turn-of-the-century Hungarian immigrants were peasants or unskilled industrial workers descended from peasant families. The experiences of one immigrant, Daniel Iváncza of Bishop, Pennsylvania, typify those of many of his contemporaries. In an account printed in 1909 in the Cleveland, Ohio, daily *Szabadság* (Liberty), a Hungarian-language newspaper, Iváncza described well the exploitation suffered by the peasantry in Hungary's semifeudal society. Back home Iváncza worked at a state-owned horse-breeding farm

An advertisement announcing transatlantic passenger voyages that appeared in a Hungarian-American newspaper in 1913. Steamship travel made possible the great wave of immigration from eastern Europe to the United States.

for 8 forints [about $3.20] per month plus board. We, 160 to 190 human beings—men and women, young and old—were housed in a . . . stall that was not even fit for hogs. . . . We tried to rest our work-weary bodies on straw that we had to collect ourselves. . . . We were lying side-by-side in that vermin-infested place, unable to rest, and without any chance to clean ourselves. . . . Most of the time we were forced to work even on Sundays and holidays. . . . When as a young boy I became sick and was unable to get up off my straw, the overseer came with a whip and lashed me. . . . Are we to be amazed that so many [peasants] become fed up not only with working for the [Hungarian] state, but with the state itself?

A slightly different view was offered by John Szabó of Chicago, Illinois, who claimed that he was driven to the United States not by privation but by the desire to live in a relatively free and uncontrolled society:

Being a thinking and a feeling man, I always had the feeling that . . . I am not quite the human being I have the right to be. . . . Thus I emigrated and learned to know America, the land of Liberty. Although initially I did suffer some privation here too . . . , I am aware that only now am I the human being that back home I only felt I had the right to be, i.e., an independent, free human being.

Iváncza and Szabó were driven to America by mistreatment and the need for a more humane existence. Others came because they could not support themselves in Hungary, believing that after a few years in America they could save enough money to return to their homeland as wealthy men. The economic deprivation of individual Hungarians mirrored problems faced by Hungary as a nation. Modernization came much later to Hungary than to western Europe. Large-scale industrialization did not take place until the last third of the 19th century. Although the Industrial Revolution created new economic opportunity in Europe, it also caused widespread social upheaval, and Hungary was no exception. With the development of factories came the need for industrial laborers, many of whom moved to large towns and cities from the impoverished countryside.

Most of the new urban industrial labor force were peasants with a shared set of beliefs. Intensely religious, they tended to be very deferential to people of authority and viewed their social superiors with both envy and awe. At the same time, they distrusted the educated classes and viewed outsmarting or upstaging them as an act of heroism. So ingrained was this attitude in the beliefs of the villagers that a successful swindling or besting of the members of the upper classes often was incorporated into their folktales. The adventures of such "smart peasants" are among the best-loved stories in the Hungarian peasant tradition. Recited again and again by the villagers with considerable relish, these folktales gave them a feeling of worth and power and nurtured within them a belief that ultimately nothing was impossible, a sentiment that would serve them well in the New World.

This family came to the United States sometime during the first decade of the 20th century, which was the peak period of Hungarian immigration.

Interwar Immigration

Hungarian immigration slowed drastically during and after World War I, and it never resumed at its former rate. There were many reasons for this, but the most decisive factor was the United States's decision to close its doors to mass immigration. In the 1920s the U.S. Congress, reflecting popular opinion that immigrants took away jobs and were somehow a threat to the American way of life, established strict annual quotas for the immigration of all nationalities. The number of Hungarians allowed to legally enter the United States each year was reduced to 5,747 in 1921 and to 473 in 1924.

Although the number of Hungarians allowed into the United States was diminished, the desire to immigrate remained great. Many Hungarians chose to enter the United States illegally during this time. The number of illegal immigrants—most of whom came

over the virtually open borders of Canada or Mexico—
is difficult to estimate, but at least one authority claims
that the number of illegal immigrants from Hungary
during the interwar years almost equaled the number
of legal entrants. Taking into account repatriation, or
those immigrants who returned home, Hungary's loss
in the years between 1920 and 1941 was somewhere
between 145,000 and 150,000 people. Perhaps less than
a third of these—or about 44,000 in all—wound up in
the United States. That figure was supplemented,
however, by Hungarian immigrants from countries,
including Czechoslovakia, Romania, and Yugoslavia,
that had been carved out of what had once been Austria-Hungary.

Most of these Hungarians chose to emigrate because of political turbulence in the homeland. Hungary
faced significant economic problems because its dis-
memberment after World War I cost it most of its natural resources and markets. At the same time, it was
inundated by hundreds of thousands of political refugees who were fleeing from the territories that had
once fallen within Hungary's domain. The depressed
Hungarian economy was scarcely able to provide for
its own remaining citizens, let alone the refugees.
Chaos, poverty, and much human misery were the
result. These problems would have been difficult to
solve had the country's leaders been effective, but
most of them made no real effort to revive the economy. Instead, they left most of interwar Hungary's
economic problems unresolved. Hardship convinced
many Hungarians to try their luck abroad.

Many of them came from the ranks of the skilled
workers and technical intelligentsia, although they
were still outnumbered by peasants by at least three
or four to one. By the 1930s, their ranks were swelled
by some of the country's most highly educated intellectuals, who fled because of their disagreement with
the country's right-wing political leadership and the
rise in anti-Semitism. By driving away its Jewish citizens, Hungary deprived itself of some of its most brilliant minds, including the internationally known
scientists who subsequently became the innovators of
America's atomic age and computer revolution.

Because the exclusionary American immigration laws of the 1920s prevented most of Hungary's interwar immigrants from entering the United States, an increasing number of them went to various other European or New World countries. Some 33,000 of them entered Canada, raising that country's Hungarian population to nearly 55,000 in 1941. It was these newcomers who laid the foundations of the Hungarian-Canadian community.

Post–World War II Immigration

Hungarian immigration to North America surged again after World War II. Recognizing that the problem of the war's displacement of huge segments of the European population required special solutions, the U.S. Congress passed several special laws that permitted a number of so-called displaced persons, or refugees, to enter the United States outside the limits of the quota system. On the basis of these laws, at least 60,000 additional Hungarian immigrants entered the United States as political exiles.

Many of these newcomers came to the United States and Canada not out of any real desire to immigrate but because postwar conditions in Hungary and central Europe left them few alternatives. The post–World War II immigrants were drawn from all levels of society and included former inmates of German concentration camps and, some years later, refugees of the Hungarian revolution of 1956. In the first 4 decades after World War II, about 110,000 Hungarians settled in the United States, and approximately 60,000 settled in Canada.

In the late 1940s and early 1950s about 5,500 Hungarian displaced persons—approximately one-third of the number who made their way to the United States—emigrated to Canada. They were followed in the late 1950s by about 38,000 "freedom fighters" or "fifty-sixers," whose number approximated that of their fellow revolutionaries who ended up in the United States. They in turn were followed by a trickle of political and economic immigrants, amounting only to a few hundred per year during the 1960s to the 1980s.

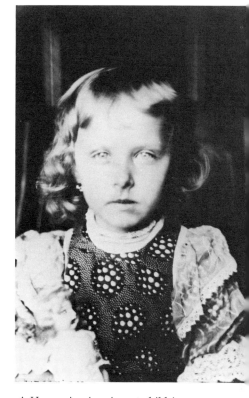

A Hungarian immigrant child in traditional dress at Ellis Island, around 1910. Located in Upper New York Bay, Ellis Island served as the United States's major immigration station between 1892 and 1943. Having left their homeland and braved the journey across the Atlantic, immigrants endured further anxiety at Ellis Island as they waited to be admitted to the United States.

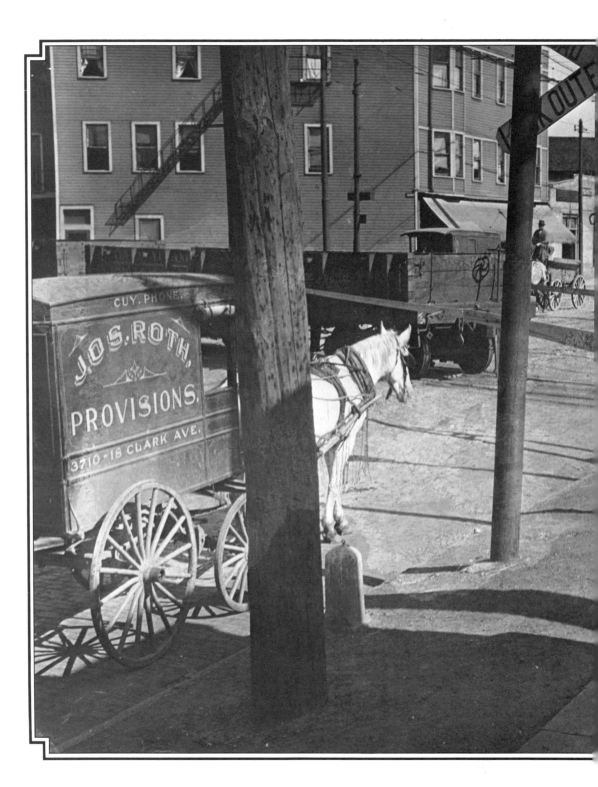

Buckeye Road in Cleveland, Ohio, about 1910. The Buckeye Road Hungarian community is perhaps the best-known Little Hungary in North America. Isolated by language, customs, and beliefs, newly arrived Hungarian immigrants often formed their own communities to help them cope with their new environment.

MAKING A NEW WORLD

I t is the descendants of the turn-of-the-century peasant immigrants who make up the bulk of the nearly 1.8 million Americans who claimed full or partial Hungarian origin in the 1980 U.S. Census. These immigrants brought with them their own customs, beliefs, and language, all of which labeled them as very different from their new American neighbors. Like other immigrant groups, Hungarians reacted to the strangeness of their new environment by creating their own enclaves that duplicated the village life they had left behind. Little Hungaries sprang up in many northeastern cities in the United States, including New York City; Philadelphia, Pennsylvania; Pittsburgh, Pennsylvania; and Bridgeport, Connecticut; as well as in such midwestern urban centers as Cleveland, Ohio; Chicago, Illinois; South Bend, Indiana; and Detroit, Michigan.

The most important institutions of this isolated Hungarian-American world were the churches and the fraternal associations of the immigrants and, to a lesser degree, the Hungarian-American newspapers. The churches and the fraternal societies were established by the peasant immigrants themselves, the former with the help of dedicated clergymen who regarded service in America as a kind of missionary work. In most instances, newspapers were founded by the handful of educated Hungarians who were among the great wave of pre–World War I immigration. Hungarian-language newspapers filled a need for information written in a language the immigrants could understand and provided educated immigrants with interesting professional jobs unavailable to them outside the Hungarian community.

The Workplace

Work defined the daily life of most Hungarian immigrants. Although America appeared a promised land from the far side of the Atlantic, new arrivals soon learned that the steel mills and coal mines of the industrial Northeast, where most of them settled, could be a landscape of misery and exploitation. Only the belief that they could earn from 5 to 10 times as much as they did back home kept them in the United States, but even this expectation was based on misinformation. The average immigrant worker earned $413 a year in 1910, a sum that likely appeared a fortune to a Hungarian, particularly if he calculated his income in his native currency, but that in the United States barely provided enough income to survive. In order to make even that much, the typical immigrant—a young, sin-

(continued on page 57)

Hungarian immigrants at work in a Connecticut factory in the early 20th century. Largely unskilled and uneducated, most of the first wave of Hungarian immigrants worked in factories, mills, and mines.

HERITAGE AND HEROISM

Dressed in authentic Hungarian blouses, a mother and daughter examine painted eggs, one of the many traditional Hungarian crafts on display at the opening of the Hungarian Heritage Center in New Brunswick, New Jersey (overleaf), while a young girl (below) watches the Hungarian Scouts Folk Dance Group perform a Maypole dance (at right) during a Hungarian-American parade. Festivals and parades are just some of the events at which Hungarian Americans come together to remember their roots and celebrate their heritage.

Magdolna Tong (at far right, dressed in traditional clothing) made her way to the United States following the unsuccessful revolution of 1956. Earlier, during World War II, she saved several individuals from imprisonment in Nazi concentration camps. In the United States, she had a successful career as an acrobat and performed with many beloved entertainers, including Bob Hope, Benny Goodman, and Mae West.

In many cities in North America, Hungarian Americans have formed cultural groups to maintain and celebrate the artistic achievements of their native land. These organizations often meet at a dance competition called a pontozók. At the pontozók held in New Brunswick, New Jersey, in 1985, the dances performed included couple dances (below and at upper right) and a men's shepherd dance (lower right).

Hungarian Catholics in New York City meet after mass each Sunday to prepare a traditional Hungarian meal and to socialize (at left). At an annual Hungarian festival held in New Brunswick, New Jersey, volunteers from church groups bake pastries to sell, such as nut- and poppy seed–filled kalacs and beigli (above). As a group, Hungarians have been highly successful at striking a balance between assimilating into North American culture and still preserving traditions from the old country.

Two members of the Hungarian-American community, one from the oldest generation, one from the youngest, enjoy a Hungarian festival in Passaic, New Jersey. Older generations of Hungarian Americans can take pride in passing on to new generations not only the history of their native land but also a legacy of significant achievements in North America.

Most of the first Hungarian immigrants were single men who worked in factories or mines. They often lived together in boardinghouses.

(continued from page 48)

gle man in his twenties—had to work between 53.7 and 63.1 hours per week in the factories, and even more in the steel mills, where the workweek often lasted all 7 days and a workday lasted 12 hours.

The turn-of-the-century immigrants were forced to survive under conditions so harsh that only their belief in a brighter and better future was able to keep them going. Contemporary sources—including newspapers, official reports, memorial albums, and private letters— are filled with the details of the gruesome industrial accidents that claimed the limbs or lives of many thousands of immigrants every year. Between 1880 and 1900, 35,000 died while working in factories or steel mills. Another 536,000 sustained serious injuries. Most of these accidents were attributed to the absence of even the most elementary protective measures. Others resulted from the immigrants' inability to read and to comprehend even the few existing warning signs that were posted in the mines and factories.

If the situation was dangerous in the factories and steel mills, it was equally perilous in the coal mines, another common source of employment for Hungarian immigrants. Early-20th-century Hungarian-American newspapers and memorial albums are replete with the details of mining accidents. This is particularly true of the *Magyar Bányászlap* (Hungarian Miner's News) of

A Hungarian miner's wife in West Virginia brings home coal for her stove at the height of the Great Depression. Although they did not work in the mines or mills, the wives of Hungarian immigrants toiled just as hard as their husbands.

Detroit, which faithfully recorded the death of thousands of untrained Hungarian immigrants in the mines of southwestern Pennsylvania, southeastern Ohio, and northern West Virginia. One of the worst accidents, which occurred in Jacobs Creek, Pennsylvania, in December 1907, was the third such accident in as many weeks in the Pittsburgh area. The Jacobs Creek accident claimed the lives of 95 Hungarians, including several youngsters under 15 years of age. When at the request of the Austro-Hungarian consul in Pittsburgh, the coroner of Allegheny County, Joseph G. Armstrong, looked into some of the allegations of unsafe working conditions, he arrived at the following general conclusions:

> The number of Hungarians who are killed in the factories in and around Pittsburgh is really phenomenal. My circumspect and thorough inquiries have led me to conclude that the lives of immigrants working in these factories and mines merit less attention than do the well-being of horses and mules. Not even the Negro slaves in the South received worse treatment during the darkest period of slavery than do the Hungarians nowadays in these factories.

At Home

During the hours they were not in the mills or mines, home life often offered little solace to the early Hungarian immigrants. Because most were single men, they lacked the consolations of marriage and family life. Whether residents of mining towns or large industrial cities, they generally lived in squalid boardinghouses, often owned by the company for which they worked, where they usually paid a monthly rent for their room, board, and such other needs as washing and cleaning. Not until after they brought their sweethearts, wives, or families to America did they move into better quarters; and not until they decided to stay permanently in North America did they attempt to buy their own homes. In most cases, immigrants did not make that decision until the 1920s. In

the meantime, their lives revolved around the society of the rooming houses.

Of the many official documents, the one that best describes the immigrants' way of life in the company-owned boardinghouses typical of the late 1800s and early 1900s was prepared by a special committee of the U.S. Department of Labor in the year 1890:

> The workers employed here are almost all Hungarians. . . . They are unassuming. . . . They resolve their lodging collectively: 30–45 men find a suitable house together and elect a *burdos gazda* [boarding master]. His job is to get provisions, pay the rent, and keep the accounts. At the end of each month all members of the group pay their part of the total expenses, plus 1.5 or 2 dollars for the wife of the burdos gazda, who cooks and cleans. . . . Everyone provides his own bedding.

This construction crew, consisting of Hungarians and Slovaks, built a power station near Montreal, Canada, in 1928. All of the men standing on the scaffolding were from the Hungarian village of Végardó. The unskilled laborers were paid 25 cents an hour; the skilled laborers, 30 cents.

Not all Hungarian immigrants worked in mines or mills, as this photo of Hungarian farm workers in the Lackawanna Valley of Pennsylvania demonstrates. Men, women, and children worked together in the fields.

The furniture is poor, consisting of home-made tables, benches . . . and beds fabricated out of old boards. . . . 4–10 men sleep in a room. Once a month, on pay day, they collectively buy a barrel of beer for 3 dollars . . . and drink it up together. . . . They usually have one decent suit besides their work clothes.

By the early 20th century, it was more common for the burdos gazda to own his own boardinghouse rather than to run one owned by a factory or mining company. He was almost always a married man whose wife served as the *burdos asszony* (boarding mistress). Her duties included cleaning, washing, ironing, mending, cooking, packing the lunch buckets, keeping financial records, serving as the boarders' banker, and performing many other chores that made her life almost unbearable. For example, the burdos asszony was often obliged to wash and rub down the backs of the returning workers and at times even to serve as mistress for one or several of them.

As described by an observer in 1909, the immigrant boardinghouse "is the strangest community, the most unusual republic, whose president is the boarding mistress [and] whose subjects enjoy equal privileges [with the husband]—usually with his knowledge and in front of him." No wonder that in those days the boardinghouses were the scenes of much violence and many family tragedies, including murder. But as noted in the December 19, 1913, issue of the *South Bendi Magyar Tudósító* (South Bend Hungarian Informer), these relationships were the products of situations where "a working-age husband was forced to emigrate in the prime of his life, leaving his blooming [wife] at home. While he yearned over here, she was languishing back home. . . . Often, the end of the story was that their instincts got the best of them. And in most instances this was followed by conflicts and by bloody tragedies."

Hungarian Americans adopted more wholesome living and working habits after deciding to settle permanently in America. Most moved out of remote mining towns to settle in the neighboring cities. They

Unlike their counterparts in the United States, the first Hungarian immigrants to Canada headed west, to the prairies of Saskatchewan, where there was ample farmland available. Dr. Frank Hoffman was a Hungarian-American missionary in Saskatchewan in the early 1900s.

found jobs in factories, shops, and service establishments and gradually bought or built their own houses in the working-class neighborhoods of their home cities. One result of the internal migration and upward mobility of the Hungarian Americans was the birth of the so-called Little Hungaries of New York, Cleveland, Chicago, and dozens of other northeastern cities. These came into being during the 1920s, and they all constituted self-contained worlds, with their own Hungarian churches, shops, businesses, clubs, bars, and cultural and political organizations.

Perhaps the best-known and most self-sufficient Little Hungary in North America was the Buckeye Road Hungarian community of Cleveland, Ohio. Founded before World War I, it enjoyed its heyday during the 1920s and 1930s and a resurgence during

The American South was never a center of Hungarian settlement, but this Hungarian-American family farmed a spread in Louisiana in the early days of the 20th century.

the 1950s and early 1960s. Its last 15 years of revitalization were spurred by the infusion of post–World War II political immigrants. Occupying an area nearly 40 city blocks in length and between 20 and 25 blocks in width, the Lower and Upper Buckeye Road Hungarian neighborhoods were filled with thousands of neatly kept family homes. This environment elevated the Hungarian immigrants above the squalor of the boardinghouses and placed them squarely into the mainstream of American life.

As they moved into the working-class neighborhoods of American cities, the Hungarian immigrants also began to shed their image as greenhorn "Hunkies," the taunt most frequently hurled at them. (Although derived from *Hungarian*, the word *Hunky* was eventually applied to most east European immigrants.) Although most of these peasant immigrants were never able to learn correct English, they began to dress, look, and act the part of "real" Americans. Most were supported in this endeavor by the Hungarian clubs, churches, and fraternal organizations that helped steer them toward assimilation.

Fraternal Associations

Life was so harsh for the turn-of-the-century immigrants that many thousands never survived to tell about it. Those who fared best did so with the help of their churches and fraternal associations. These organizations served as "homes away from home" and were sources of social and psychological support for the immigrants.

Of these two institutions, the fraternal organizations were the most important. Initially, they functioned as self-help societies that donated money, collected as dues from members, to the families of sick workers. They also bore the cost of funerals, which were often too expensive for families to afford on their own. Later, fraternal societies also offered immigrants a haven from the cruel life of the factories.

The first of these associations were established during the 1850s and 1860s by immigrants fleeing the failed revolution of 1848–49, but the political focus of

AZ
"EGYESÜLT MAGYAR POLGÁRI
SZÖVETSÉG"

ALAPSZABÁLYAI

"I pledge allegiance to the Flag of the United States of America and to the Republic for which it stands, one Nation, indivisible, with Liberty and Justice for all."

BY-LAWS
of the
UNITED MAGYARS' CIVIC
ASSOCIATION

A copy of the bylaws of the United Magyars' Civic Association. *Such fraternal organizations helped immigrants adjust to life in their new country.*

such early organizations left them ill equipped to fulfill the needs of the late-19th-century economic immigrants. The latter thus found it necessary to establish their own associations, which they did during the 1880s, when nearly a dozen Hungarian fraternal societies came into being. These were followed by hundreds of others over the course of the next 30 years. By 1910, Hungarian Americans had 1,339 such associations. Whereas some existed only to provide benefits during illness, others were social and cultural organizations, both with and without affiliations to such religious and political organizations as the Catholic church and various socialist and workers' movements.

Most of the organizations were small and scattered throughout hundreds of Hungarian settlements in 28 different states. Some of the larger settlements had dozens of such organizations. The leading centers were Cleveland, home to 81 fraternal societies, and New York City, which boasted 78 such groups. Each of these urban centers also offered several competing sick-benefit societies, of which only a few survived into the 1920s.

The most successful of the fraternal associations was the Verhovay Aid Society, founded in 1886 in Hazleton, Pennsylvania. Over time, this organization grew into the largest and most significant Hungarian fraternal association in North America. Today it is known as the William Penn Association. Located in Pittsburgh, it has 70,000 members, $80 million in assets, and is more than twice as large as its nearest major rival, the Hungarian Reformed Federation of America, founded in 1896.

The local branches of the Hungarian fraternal societies also served as instruments of democracy, offering Hungarian peasants, often for the first time in their life, the chance to act politically on their own behalf, in the form of voting and running for society office. Since the Hungarians did not become citizens in large numbers until the 1920s, the fraternals offered them an early opportunity to learn about American-style democratic procedures. In this way the fraternals encouraged pride among the working-class immigrants and helped mold them into citizens with rights and privileges akin to those of the upper classes in Hungary.

Churches and Religious Denominations

The Hungarian churches in America rivaled the fraternal societies in importance to the immigrant community. Perhaps even more than the fraternals, the churches gave the immigrants a feeling of security. The congregations served as centers of the immigrants' religious, cultural, and social lives and as the perpetuators of Hungarian national traditions. Much as they had been in Hungarian villages, clergymen were regarded as highly revered paternal figures who protected and advised their flock.

Religious leaders such as Zsigmond Laky, a Hungarian-American Protestant minister, were esteemed members of Hungarian communities in North America.

In North America, Hungarian churches combined two traditional village institutions: the church and the inn. In Hungary, the churches were simply places of worship, while the village inns provided centers of male social activities. There men met to eat and drink, exchange gossip, and debate local and national politics. In America, these two village institutions were merged. The inn was moved down to the church basement, in the process losing its exclusivity as a predominantly male bastion and also much of its boisterousness. At the same time, the intrusion of the secular world relieved the churches of some of their sanctity and the clergymen of some of their aura of infallibility.

The restructured churches remained important institutions, however. In addition to serving their congregants, Hungarian-American clergymen remained the primary exponents and protectors of the Hungarian national spirit, Hungarian language, and Hungarian culture in America. They stood in the forefront of the struggle to establish Hungarian schools, religious and cultural associations, and even Hungarian newspapers in the United States and Canada. Without the dedication of the clergymen, Hungarian nationalism might have perished among the immigrant generation and their native-born offspring.

The two largest Christian denominations among the immigrants were Roman Catholicism and Calvinism (Reformed Church). The first Hungarian Catholic parish established in America was the Saint Elizabeth of Hungary Church in Cleveland, Ohio, founded in 1893. The founder, Monsignor Charles Boehm, is widely regarded as the father of Hungarian Catholicism in the United States. One year after establishing Saint Elizabeth's, Boehm began the first Hungarian-Catholic fraternal association, Amerikai Magyar Katolikus Egylet (American Hungarian Catholic Society), and that same year he printed the first Hungarian-Catholic newspaper, *Katolikus Magyarok Vasárnapja* (Catholic Hungarians' Sunday).

Boehm's counterpart among the Calvinists was Reverend Gustav Jurányi, who founded the first Hungarian Reformed congregation in 1890 in Cleveland,

Ohio. The most outstanding representative of Hungarian Calvinism in America, however, was Reverend Sándor Kalassay. Born in 1869, he came to the United States in 1895 and soon after became the founder of a number of Calvinist institutions and organizations, including the still-existing American Hungarian Reformed Federation, established in 1896.

The Hungarian Lutherans, Eastern Orthodox Catholics, Baptists, Unitarians, Pentecostalists, and Jews also established their own churches, prayer houses, and synagogues. Being much fewer in number, their congregations were smaller and their influence on Hungarian-American life more limited. Of all the denominations, Hungarian Jews were the first to establish their own place of worship, the B'nai Jeshurun Hungarian Jewish Orthodox Synagogue of Cleveland, Ohio, which was founded in 1868.

Journalism, Literature, and Language

The Hungarian-language press proved nearly as important as churches and fraternal organizations to the Hungarian-American community. The immigrants' primary source of information was newspapers, especially three Hungarian-language dailies: the Cleveland-based *Szabadság* and the New York-based *Amerikai Magyar Népszava* (American Hungarian People's Voice) and *Új Előre* (New Forward).

Hungarian newspapers served to help unite the scattered Hungarian communities in North America. They kept the spirit of Hungarian nationalism alive, disseminated information about events in the mother country, and promoted civic consciousness.

In order to be accessible to the majority of the immigrants, most Hungarian-American publications of the late 19th and mid-20th centuries printed articles written specifically for an uneducated readership. Virtually all the newspapers trumpeted Hungarian nationalism and filled their pages with local social and cultural activities connected with the fraternal associations, churches, and other immigrant organizations. At the same time, they refrained from editorializing about American life outside the confines of Hungarian communities in the United States and Canada. This

A Hungarian-American Reformed church in Connecticut. The church served immigrants both as a house of worship and a place for socializing.

Szabadság (Liberty) of Cleveland, Ohio, is the largest Hungarian-American newspaper. The front page of the April 10, 1933, issue uses a cartoon to comment on high meat prices. Hungarian-language newspapers helped unite Hungarian communities throughout North America.

timid and rather provincial style of journalism changed after World War II, when postwar political immigrants greatly enlivened Hungarian-American periodicals.

The Struggle to Survive

The immigrants' attachment to Hungarian-American newspapers reflected the more intense allegiance they felt toward their native land. This fierce loyalty was encouraged by the Hungarian government, which in 1905 launched a national propaganda campaign known as American Action. The government implemented the American Action program by subsidizing some of the more influential newspaper editors, clergy, and advocates of the Hungarian-American community. Those working for the government encouraged passionate feelings of nationalism among Hungarian Americans by equating the love of Hungary with the love of God. Like their brethren in Hungary, they also recited with passion the Hungarian Creed (Magyar Hiszekegy):

> I believe in one God! I believe in one Country! I believe in one divine, eternal truth! I believe in the resurrection of Hungary!

While this effort achieved some success, in the long run it was doomed to failure because the majority of the immigrants chose to stay in America and Canada and to become citizens of their adopted countries. Over time, as the first wave of Hungarian immigrants raised children in the United States and Canada, their ties to the mother country grew weaker. Of course, the immigrants retained great affection for their homeland no matter how Americanized they and their families eventually became.

The unveiling of a statue commemorating Hungarian nationalist leader Lajos Kossuth in New York City in 1928. Many Hungarian immigrants remained active in the politics of their homeland, supporting movements for an independent Hungary.

The dual loyalty of Hungarian Americans posed a dilemma for many of them during World War I, when Hungary sided with Germany against the Allied powers. As noted by a contemporary observer in the 25th anniversary edition of the daily *Amerikai Magyar Népszava* in 1924: "The fact that fate has given . . . [us] two homelands now fell upon us like a lash that tore into our very souls." During the war, Hungarians found themselves regarded with suspicion and even hatred by other Americans. That particular situation improved little after the war. Although the hostility toward them subsided somewhat, Hungarian Americans felt deeply the loss of the Austro-Hungarian Empire. For the next two decades they joined with their relatives, friends, and compatriots back in Hungary in the struggle to revise the postwar treaties and redraw the new national borders. Hungarian Americans sometimes seemed more interested in the politics of their homeland than in the current events that occupied the minds of most Americans or Canadians. During the 1920s they conducted mass rallies in such cities as New York, Buffalo, Philadelphia, Cleveland, Chicago, and Pittsburgh and also sent a steady stream of petitions to various American political leaders, the U.S. Congress, and the White House.

Despite this flurry of activism on behalf of the old country, many Hungarians sought and acquired U.S. citizenship during this time. Whereas before World War I only 15 percent of Hungarian immigrants were U.S. citizens, by 1920 this number rose to 20.4 percent; by 1930 it had reached 55.7 percent, and by 1940 it had bettered the 80 percent mark. Many Hungarian Americans became citizens by virtue of being born on American soil. As more people of Hungarian descent were born in the United States—and as the quotas of the 1920s barred thousands of Hungarians from entering the United States each year—American citizens accounted for an ever-growing percentage of the Hungarian-American community. In 1930 that community was about evenly divided between native born and immigrants, but by 1940 the native born outnumbered the immigrants by a ratio of three to two.

A Hungarian-American woman poses in a traditional Hungarian costume in the early 1900s. Traditions began to fade as the children of Hungarian immigrant parents adopted the customs, beliefs, and language of Canada and the United States.

Intergenerational Conflicts

The change in composition of the Hungarian community in America was accompanied by the conflicts that often arise as a result of the pressure or need to assimilate. The community grew divided between those who were citizens and those who were not. On a smaller scale, individual families and the community at large experienced a rift between older members and the younger generation, which considered itself Americanized and fought to be accepted as such by other Americans. Their very first weapon in this struggle

The christening of a Hungarian-American infant in New York City. Hungarian Americans still strive to maintain a balance between assimilating into North American society and preserving the customs of their heritage.

was the rejection of the customs, traditions, and even the language of their parents, which they regarded in many cases as inferior to American traditions and the English language. Whereas the immigrant generation had been determined to hold on to that which branded it as Hungarian, members of succeeding generations often resolved to shed all that identified them as anything other than American.

The growing chasm between American-born Hungarians and their parents took a great toll on the older generation. They tried to revive their children's interest in Hungarian culture but met with only limited success. Ultimately nothing could prevent the younger generation's Americanization and their embracing of English as their primary language. Given these realities, many of the Hungarian churches, organizations, and newspapers began using both languages in the 1930s, and by the 1950s the majority of them had ceased to employ Hungarian at all. Had not a new generation of immigrants arrived following World War II, Hungarian culture and the Hungarian language would probably have disappeared altogether from American society.

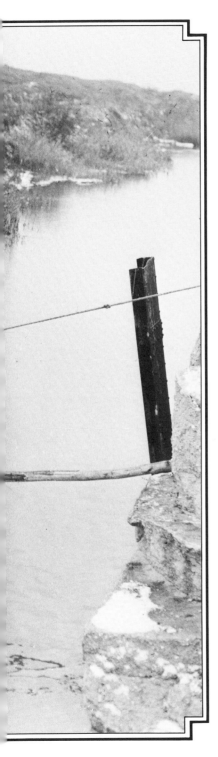

Using an unsteady bridge consisting of a long pole and a rope, Hungarians cross a border canal into Austria in November 1956. Despite attempts by the Soviet Union to block all routes out of Hungary during the 1956 revolution, more than 200,000 people escaped.

THE POLITICAL IMMIGRANTS

N orth America received its second large infusion of Hungarian immigrants immediately before and after World War II. Most of these were men and women who had been driven from their homeland by the fear of political persecution. In the 1930s the United States opened its doors to a small group of highly trained Hungarian scientists, artists, and intellectuals, among them a number of current or future Nobel Prize winners. Those Hungarians who arrived following World War II—about 17,000 in all were admitted under the Displaced Persons Acts of 1948 and 1950, and 40,000 as refugees from the failed revolution of 1956—represented a considerable portion of interwar and postwar Hungary's social and political elite. Although the later arrivals constituted only 15 to 20 percent of the total number of Hungarians who immigrated to the United States, their status as educated members of the middle and upper classes untainted, as were many of the displaced persons, by association with Nazi Germany, enabled them to win almost immediate acceptance into American society, and many made enormous contributions to the country that had welcomed them.

Educated immigrants have almost always accounted for a majority of all Hungarians in Canada, largely because the high point of Hungarian immigration to that country did not occur until the decades following World War II. Canada welcomed some 9,500 displaced persons (DPs), and an additional 36,700 Hungarians were admitted in the aftermath of the 1956 revolution.

The Displaced Persons

The displaced persons were those dislocated by the violence and upheaval of World War II. They perhaps best fit the category of political immigrants and represented a broad cross section of Hungarian society. A significant portion of them were middle- and upper-level bureaucrats and army officers. At the same time, displaced persons included less favored members of Hungarian society, such as Jews and members of political-opposition groups. Some of these immigrated after their liberation from concentration camps in 1945; others came to North America after Hungary's postwar coalition governments gave way to one-party rule by the Communists in 1948.

Most of the displaced persons spent the years immediately following World War II in various German and Austrian refugee camps, waiting and hoping for political changes that would permit them to return to their country as "liberators." As described by Gertrude Ely, an official observer for the United Nations International Refugee Organization (IRO), in the April 1948 issue of *Survey Graphic*, their living conditions were something less than comfortable:

> The displaced persons usually are housed in stark, unfriendly former German barracks or partially damaged factory buildings, rarely with heat, without running water or hot water and often with no soap. Yet these people and their children manage to put up a miraculously good appearance. Privacy has been impossible during years of war and "liberation." The only partitions in most of the long, bare rooms are made by hanging blankets or paper or bits of clothing on a

Fiorello La Guardia (right, front), mayor of New York City, and a passel of Hungarian-American children celebrate the donation of 10 ambulances to the Red Cross by Hungarian Americans in 1943. The uneasy alliance between Hungary and Nazi Germany placed Hungarian Americans in a precarious position during World War II.

string. Even though families and single men and girls live in these screened-off places they appreciate pathetically the small amount of privacy they indicate.

The sad situation of the displaced persons was further complicated by the presence of many old people and small children in their midst. Thousands of these children were orphans who had either been taken from their parents or lost their elders during the chaotic final phase of the war. They often remained in the camps for years, surviving with only minimal help from the war victims or from various international welfare organizations.

Ultimately, many of the displaced persons immigrated to the United States, Canada, Australia, Israel, and such Latin American countries as Argentina, Brazil, and Venezuela. Just preparing for emigration, transit, and arrival was in itself a trying experience. Most countries wanted only healthy immigrants young enough to find jobs and support themselves financially. Even these choice candidates were rigorously screened before they were admitted to the United States. Many were forced to leave their elderly or ill relatives behind in Europe. Many émigrés later criticized the selection process as being like a slave market in which only the finest chattel were chosen. The ar-

In New York City, Hungarian Americans, both Jewish and non-Jewish, protest Nazi persecution of Hungarian Jews. Horthy's government was able to protect Jews from Hitler's extermination plan until the Germans invaded Hungary in March 1944 and began to deport Jews to concentration camps. The protesters are wearing armbands featuring the Magen David, a symbol of Judaism.

rival of a group of displaced persons in New York City was described by Paul E. Deutschman in the November 1948 issue of *The American* magazine as follows:

> I was at the New York docks one blustery day a few months ago watching a boatload of the DP-immigrants passing through Customs. They were people who had been penned up in camps for years. They had lost everything—including their homes, their native lands (fully three-fourths of all DPs are nationals of Communist-dominated lands who can't or won't go home), and often their entire families. Now, as might be expected, they were anxious to forget the grim Past and begin living again, in the hopeful Future.

The life of the displaced persons in their new countries was far from easy. They were received with suspicion by the nations that had fought against their homeland during the war; they found it difficult to get along with the earlier immigrants, who generally came from much lower social classes than they themselves; they often lacked transferable diplomas and professional certification that would win them employment appropriate to their level of education; and many of them felt reluctant to assimilate into U.S. and Canadian society because they dreamed of returning to a liberated Hungary.

The cold reception displaced persons received in America was a small obstacle in comparison with their struggle to obtain employment commensurate with their education and training. Many were confined to working at occupations far below their educational and intellectual capabilities because their degrees from Hungary's military academies and law schools—the latter being virtually mandatory in the old country for all middle- to upper-level bureaucrats—meant little to North American employers. Displaced persons found that they had two options: to undergo training in a new profession—a course that few of them chose—or to seek employment as unskilled workers. In Cleveland during the 1950s, for example, three former generals and scores of former government officials worked as common laborers.

Even if somehow spared the problem of obtaining employment suitable to their education, most of the displaced persons still faced other difficulties in adjusting to American society. In Hungary they had enjoyed great social prestige, political power, and

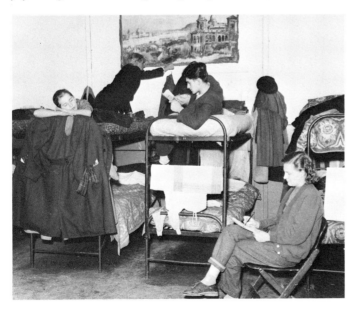

A typical room in the refugee camp at Wiener Neustadt in Austria. The former Russian army barracks were used to house Hungarian refugees awaiting passage to the United States in 1956.

Frank Lieber, chairman of the Canadian Hungarian Relief Fund, signs a check that will assist political refugees fleeing Hungary in the wake of the 1956 revolution.

financial security, but in the United States and Canada these same individuals were now members of democratic societies in which social position and aristocratic lineage counted for little. Many Hungarians resented the notion of an egalitarian society, and they regarded the average North American as gauche, naive, and ill bred. Such Hungarian émigrés survived their exile in the United States by creating a separate world in which they preserved the formal European culture they had always known.

The Fifty-sixers

The fifty-sixers, or freedom fighters, as those who came to North America in the wake of the thwarted Hungarian revolution of 1956 were called, brought with them different concerns. During that time, tens of thousands of Hungarians fled their country either voluntarily or because they were forced out. Although officially categorized as freedom fighters, only a minority among them had participated in the actual fighting, and most of them were more interested in building a better life for themselves than in transforming Hungary. They left their country simply because they were fed up with conditions there and because Hungary's borders had suddenly been opened for the first time since World War II.

Most of the approximately 40,000 fifty-sixers belonged to a class of young technocrats who had been trained as future leaders by Hungary's Communist government. Before the revolution they had been regarded as flag bearers for the new social order being built in Hungary, and as such their education differed from that of the displaced persons. Most had studied such practical fields as engineering, technology, and natural sciences.

This education prepared the fifty-sixers well for the working world of America in the 1950s. Their practical training allowed them to move easily into the American industrial establishment and enabled them to assimilate rapidly. With the exception of a small core of political activists who settled in established Hungarian-American communities, the fifty-sixers soon merged into North American society. This proved a simple matter not only because of their professional training but also because the political climate in the United States during the 1950s, characterized at times by rabid anticommunism and hostility toward the Soviet Union, ensured that the émigrés received a warm welcome from the American people. For example, those immigrants who had not yet completed their education received considerable assistance in finishing their schooling, as reported by the Committee on Educational Interchange Policy:

> From the first day of the exodus from Hungary, American educational institutions and organizations expressed their interest in helping the Hungarian students. . . . A cooperative program was established to place Hungarian students in American colleges and universities where scholarship opportunities were available. . . . To meet the students' needs for English training . . . two special centers were established and supervised by the Institute of International Education. . . . Bard College . . . accepted 325 for nine weeks, and St. Michael's College . . . approximately 100 for fifteen weeks. Financial support was obtained from the Ford and Rockefeller foundations and from the Rockefeller Brothers Fund.

Twenty-one Hungarian refugees pose beneath the nose of President Dwight D. Eisenhower's personal plane, Columbine, which brought them to the United States from Munich, West Germany, on Christmas Day, 1956. The children hold gifts from the president.

In the March 24, 1957, issue of the *New York Times*, Harrison W. Salisbury called the influx of the fifty-sixers the "most successful mass migration in American history." This was particularly true in the case of the fifty-sixer students, an unusually high number of whom won honors at America's top universities.

Perhaps because of their experiences in Hungary, many of the fifty-sixers shunned Hungarian-American communities and organizations after their arrival. Many distanced themselves further from their heritage by marrying North Americans. For a long time proportionately few fifty-sixers involved themselves in Hungarian cultural activities, but this seems to be changing. Upon reaching middle age, a significant number began to return to their Hungarian roots and for the first time found common ground with those who came before and after them.

Organizations and Politics

The first generation of Hungarian immigrants and their descendants centered their lives around churches, fraternal associations, and, in a few instances, socialist labor organizations. By contrast, the postwar political immigrants focused their attention on their own newly founded cultural and political associations. Some of the most influential of these were the Fraternal Association of Hungarian Veterans, the Royal Hungarian Gendarmerie Benevolent Association, the Hungarian Scouts in Exile, the Hungarian Freedom Fighters' Federation, and the Association of Hungarian University Students, founded by the fifty-sixers in 1957. During the 1960s the DPs and the fifty-sixers also assumed control of the American Hungarian Federation and the Hungarian Canadian Federation, umbrella organizations formed in 1906 and 1951, respectively, to protect the interests of Hungarians in North America. All of these organizations opened local branches throughout North America.

In a sense, all associations of displaced persons and fifty-sixers were political organizations, even though these organizations generally concerned themselves only with "ethnic politics" until the 1970s. For nearly 25 years after their arrival in North America, the displaced persons had little or no concern for American or Canadian domestic politics. Instead, they focused on their new government's relations with the old country.

Foremost in the minds of many was the desire to free Hungary from the Soviet bloc, an ambition fueled by the cold war between the East and West. When relations improved between the Soviet Union and the United States and Canada, many Hungarian Americans relinquished some of the animosity they felt toward the Soviet government, but this shift in attitude divided the Hungarian communities in the United States and Canada. One faction pursued a strategy of

A crowd outside the gates of Camp Kilmer, New Jersey, greets the first 60 Hungarian political refugees to arrive in America during the 1956 revolution. From November 1956 to May 1957, Camp Kilmer served as the reception center for nearly 30,000 Hungarian refugees.

confrontation toward Hungarian Communists and North American policymakers who favored peace with the Soviets. The other faction followed a conciliatory policy and supported the old country's efforts to normalize its relations with the Hungarian communities abroad as well as with the two North American governments.

This disagreement over policy toward Hungary led to bitter political struggles among Hungarian Americans and reached a climax in 1978. That year, President Jimmy Carter decided to return the Holy Crown of Saint Stephen to the Hungarian government. (The crown had been in the United States since its discovery in an abandoned mine shaft by American soldiers during the closing days of World War II.) The most vocal members of the Hungarian communities in North America regarded this as an immoral act that indicated acceptance of a regime they viewed as illegitimate. Those willing to compromise viewed Carter's gesture as a natural step toward normalization. Today, politically active Hungarian Americans have yet to fully resolve their differences on this issue.

Although divided over U.S.-Hungarian relations, all Hungarian Americans stand united in their concern for the human rights of the nearly 4 million Hungarians living in the countries surrounding Hungary, such as Romania, Czechoslovakia, the Soviet Union, and Yugoslavia. They are particularly concerned for their brethren in the first two countries, where ethnic Hungarians are harassed and subjected to forced denationalization. This concern spawned a number of organizations whose primary interest is the defense of Hungarian minorities. The most important is the Hungarian Human Rights Commission, based in New York City.

Journalism, Publishing, and Literature

The arrival of the postwar political immigrants raised the number of Hungarian-American and Hungarian-Canadian newspapers to about four dozen. These included two dailies, the Cleveland-based *Szabadság* and the New York-based *Amerikai Magyar Népszava*; the semiweekly *Kanadai Magyar Ujság* (Canadian Hungarian News), which served the mainline Hungarian-Canadian community; and numerous similar periodicals. Ninety percent of these were published in the United States, but some of the largest, most influential, and most enduring newspapers were printed in Canada. These included the *Kanadai Magyarság* (Canadian Hungarians) and the *Magyar Élet* (Hungarian Life) of Toronto. Although most of the papers represented the traditional nationalist sentiments of their editors and readers, a small but vocal minority of these publications expounded socialist views and supported political developments in post–World War II Hungary.

Most of the newspapers read by the earlier immigrants seemed naive and simplistic to the postwar wave of Hungarian newcomers, who responded by founding their own periodicals. These new organs generally preached an anticommunist line. In 1956, Hungarian journalists in the United States launched their most ambitious project to date, the *Szabad Magyarság* (Free Hungarians), a publication representing right-of-center political views. Originally slated as a daily, the newspaper never achieved the wide readership it desired and was printed only semiweekly before folding in 1962. Other influential papers included the Cleveland- and later Youngstown-based *Katolikus Magyarok Vasárnapja* (Catholic Hungarians' Sunday), the Pittsburgh-based *Magyarság* (Hungarians), and the St. Louis–based *St. Louis és Vidéke* (St. Louis and Vicinity).

But it was not until the late 1970s that Hungarian journalism strove to convey information in a disinterested and professional manner. For the first time periodicals featured balanced presentation of stories and purposely omitted the emotional language that had once characterized the Hungarian press. Some of the best known and most highly regarded of these more recent periodicals are *Itt-Ott* (Here and There) and *Szivárvány* (Rainbow), both published in the United States, and *Nyugati Magyarság* (Hungarians of the West), a Canadian publication.

Although much of Hungarian-American literature was and is available only on the pages of the com-

Hungarian Americans picket Edmonton's Ukrainian Center in December 1970 to protest Soviet control of their homeland. Many Hungarians living in North America remain committed to an independent Hungary.

munity's newspapers and periodicals, some of it also appears in book form. Because the market for such volumes is very small in the United States and Canada, most authors writing in Hungarian must subsidize the publication of their own work. Most Hungarian-American novelists and poets have not been able to earn a living solely by writing and have supported themselves by working in other fields. The sole exception to this rule may have been the internationally known playwright Ferenc Molnár, whose plays were translated and popularized during World War II.

While the greatest problem for Hungarian-American authors has always been the language barrier, most were also limited by their subject matter. Even if translated into English, their works generally failed to capture the interest and attention of the American reading public, and they remained unknown in America. Moreover, if American-born Hungarians became creative writers, they generally wrote in English and did not readily identify themselves as Hungarian writers.

As with their political orientation, most Hungarians are of a conservative bent in their artistic tastes. Modern literary methods and aims held very little appeal for the majority of immigrants, who generally read only traditional Hungarian or Hungarian-American literature. Such material is united thematically by its shared criticism of the present and idealization of the past. In recent years several avant-garde artistic schools have arisen, but their appeal is limited.

The Present and Future

In the last decade of the 20th century, the Hungarian-American community is in a state of transition. The descendants of the 19th-century immigrants are often Hungarian in name only. Most have adopted the social values of their new country and have thoroughly assimilated themselves. The postwar political immigrants of the late 1940s and 1950s were more obviously Hungarian in their language, culture, and values, but only a minority of these men and women are still alive in the late 1980s.

Most of the fifty-sixers, now well into middle age, have raised children who consider themselves American or Canadian rather than Hungarian. But, unlike any other group of Hungarian Americans, a significant portion of these offspring have established contacts with the land and culture of their ancestors and in some instances have spent time there as students. As a result, many children of the fifty-sixers have forged a new tie with their parents' homeland. In some cases they feel closer to that homeland than do their parents, who often harbor bitterness toward their native country.

The offspring of the political immigrants tend to be educated professionals, members of the middle or upper middle class. Unlike their 19th-century predecessors, who labored in factories and mines, these men and women enjoy a comfortable position in American society, and their financial security provides them with the mobility, resources, and leisure time to explore their roots. Just as they reap many benefits from their renewed association with Hungary, so, too, the country of their ancestors profits from its "wayward sons and daughters." As Hungary moves more quickly toward Westernization, it benefits from its business contacts in Western Europe and North America, many of whom are descended from Hungarian immigrants.

THE MYSTERY OF THE HUNGARIAN TALENT

Despite their relatively small numbers, it can fairly be said that Hungarian Americans have provided American society with an astonishing array of talented individuals. In journalism, a Hungarian American was one of the United States's most important newspaper publishers of the 19th century, and the prize that today still bears his name remains a symbol of journalistic and literary excellence. Hollywood, California, the legendary home of the motion picture industry, may be a quintessentially American locale, but in the infancy of the movies Hungarian Americans were among the new art's most important practitioners. The artistic flair of Hungarian Americans has been similarly demonstrated by the creations of several gifted composers, conductors, sculptors, and painters, and modern science was revolutionized by a number of brilliant Hungarian Americans, who together ushered the United States and the world into the nuclear age. Indeed, the achievements of Hungarian Americans have been so disproportionate to their relatively small numbers in comparison with other ethnic groups that more than one observer has pondered "the mystery of the Hungarian talent."

Pulitzer Apprized

The man whose name would grace the most coveted award in American journalism was only 17 when he left his native Hungary, where he had been born on April 10, 1847, in the city of Makó. After a classical education in the city of Budapest, Joseph Pulitzer left his homeland to seek his fortune in the United States, as many a young European of his day was doing. Shortly after arriving in the United States in 1864, he enlisted in the Union army and served during the last year of the Civil War. Destitution followed at war's end, until he obtained a job in St. Louis, Missouri, as a reporter on the *Westliche Post*, a German-language newspaper edited by his former commanding officer, Carl Schurz, a German immigrant who went on to become secretary of the interior. From that day on, journalism and politics would be Pulitzer's ruling passions. By 1871 he was part owner of the *Post* as well as a reforming member of the Missouri legislature. Seven years later, he purchased both the *St. Louis Dispatch* and the *St. Louis Post*, which he merged into a single publication. Pulitzer's political savvy, belief in newspapers as a democratic medium, and keen sense of the public's taste quickly made the *Post-Dispatch* the most important newspaper in the American West and one of the nation's most influential.

In 1883, Pulitzer moved his operations to New York City, where he bought the *New York World*, transforming that staid daily through the addition of photographs, comic strips, and often sensational headlines. Detractors criticized these innovations as "yellow journalism," but Pulitzer saw no contradiction between appealing to his readership and what he saw as journalism's unique mission to educate the masses. Although Pulitzer was convinced that it was the obligation of the press to inculcate civic-mindedness and patriotism in its readers as well as to show them the way to social and economic progress, he also believed that his papers had to reflect the hopes, aspirations,

Journalist and newspaper magnate Joseph Pulitzer, whose newspapers were renowned for crusading editorials and sensationalist reporting, conceived of such innovations as sports coverage, comics, and illustrations. In his will, he endowed the prestigious Pulitzer Prize, awarded each year for excellence in journalism, letters, and music.

and interests of the man in the street. This insight earned his papers a loyal following and enabled him to make a considerable fortune.

By the turn of the century, Pulitzer's eyesight was failing, and he devoted most of his energies to the future of American journalism, endowing Columbia University's School of Journalism and establishing the Pulitzer Prize, awarded for excellence in a number of journalistic, literary, and musical categories. Pulitzer also provided financial assistance to some of his compatriots, such as the great Hungarian painter Milály Munkácsy, and bequeathed large sums of money to such cultural institutions as the Philharmonic Society and the Metropolitan Museum of New York. He died on October 20, 1911, while on board his luxurious yacht, *Liberty*, off the coast of South Carolina.

The Secrets of the Atom

Perhaps no discoveries have more revolutionized the way man understands his world than those concerning atomic particles and their harnessing as a source of energy and a destructive force. No machine is more emblematic of the modern age than the computer, and there are few fields of scientific and intellectual inquiry more daunting than the theoretical mathematics that gave rise to the first computers. No recent scientific achievement better reflects humanity's innate need to explore and understand than its various ventures into space. In all these areas, Hungarian Americans, many of them political and cultural exiles from the land of

King Gustav VI of Sweden (left) presents the 1963 Nobel Prize for physics to Professor Eugene P. Wigner of Princeton University. Wigner, who arrived in the U.S. in 1933 and became an American citizen in 1937, won the prize for his basic research on the structure of the atom. Years earlier, he had been instrumental in developing the atom bomb.

their birth, were responsible for critical scientific breakthroughs and discoveries that changed modern history. It is this absolutely immense contribution of Hungarian Americans to modern science that has led observers to ask how such a relatively small group of people could give rise to so many men of genius.

The best example of this influence was the Hungarian role in the U.S. development of the atom bomb during World War II. In 1942 a Nobel Prize–winning Italian immigrant physicist working at the University of Chicago, Enrico Fermi, created the first self-sustaining nuclear reaction. One of his assistants, a Hungarian physicist named Leo Szilárd, almost immediately recognized how nuclear chain reactions could be used to create a bomb of almost immeasurable destructive force. This recognition was the first step toward the creation of the Manhattan Project. Even before Fermi's breakthrough, Szilárd and Eugene Wigner, another Hungarian scientist in exile, had set out to convince President Franklin Roosevelt of the critical necessity of developing atomic weapons. The two Hungarians enlisted the support of Albert Einstein, the world's most prominent scientist and the creator of the theory of relativity. All three were essentially pacifists, but as exiles from a Europe overrun by the madness of Hitler's nazism (Einstein was a German Jew), they recognized that atomic weapons could guarantee victory in the all but inevitable war with the Nazis, even if used only as a deterrent, and they were frightened by reports that the Germans had begun building nuclear weapons of their own. According to Laura Fermi, Enrico's widow, Einstein's famous letter of August 2, 1939, to Roosevelt, in which he urged the beginning of intensive research into atomic weaponry, was in fact written by Szilárd and Wigner and then signed by the prestigious Einstein.

Einstein's involvement certainly demanded the president's notice, and coordinated research began in earnest after Fermi's successful chain reaction. Fermi, Szilárd, and Wigner made a formidable scientific team, as their individual gifts meshed well. According to Laura Fermi, "Szilárd threw out ideas; with his practical intuition Fermi turned them into rough theories that served immediately to guide experiments; and Wigner, more patient and rigorous, refined them into mathematically cogent theories that would stand the test of time." Work on the Manhattan Project, which was directed by Robert Oppenheimer, was centered in Los Alamos, New Mexico, where Fermi, Wigner, and Szilárd were joined by dozens of other scientists, many of them refugees from war-ravaged Europe. The first successful explosion of an atom bomb took place in the desert near Alamogordo, New Mexico, on July 16, 1945. Germany had already surrendered by then, but the two atom bombs dropped on the cities of Hiroshima and Nagasaki in August 1945 hastened Japan's capitulation. Many of the scientists who worked on the Manhattan Project were appalled when they saw the physical devastation caused by the practical application of their work. Szilárd, for one, was noted in later years for his opposition to the use of nuclear weapons. Another Hungarian immigrant, Edward Teller, took the Manhattan Project's research one step further and is renowned as the father of the hydrogen bomb.

Atomic weaponry is merely one area in which Hungarian-American scientists have made invaluable contributions. Theodor von Kármán is sometimes called the father of supersonic flight, and John von Neumann, the creator of cybernetics and much early computer theory, was simply the greatest mathematician of his day. Szilárd, Wigner, Teller, von Kármán, and von Neumann made possible America's scientific preeminence during the war and in the decades immediately afterward and ushered in the atomic and computer age.

To these may be added the names of dozens of other Hungarian-American scientists, whose contributions may not have been as spectacular or well known but were valuable nonetheless. These include the Nobel laureates George de Hevessy, Albert Szent-Györgyi, and George von Békésy, who were honored for their research in chemistry and medicine; the famed mathematicians George Pólya and Gábor Szegö, who made Stanford University in California one of the world's premier centers of mathematical learning; the atomic physicist Zoltán Bay, whose research led to the development of the radio telescope; the Nobel laureate Dennis Gabor, who was working on the electronic microscope in England when he almost accidentally invented the holograph; the much younger John G. Kemény of Dartmouth College, an exponent of finite mathematics and its application at Dartmouth; such second-generation Nobel laureates in chemistry as Daniel C. Gajdusek and Andrew W. Schally of the United States and John C. Polányi of Canada; and applied scientists such as Peter C. Goldmark, who, while employed at RCA, invented the long-playing phonograph record, developed the first practical color-television system, and introduced the electronic video recording system.

In general, the lives of virtually all of these world-renowned Hungarian scientists share several characteristics. Most of them were born near the turn of the century in the Hungarian capital of Budapest. They were all brought up in well-to-do middle-class families and were the spiritual children of a city in the midst of a cultural and intellectual golden age that made it one of the showplaces of Europe. All were the products of the phenomenally successful Hungarian secondary school system—many of them graduates of the Fasor Evangelical Gymnasium of Budapest—which had few parallels on the Continent. Because of the scarcity of available positions at Hungary's three universities, many of the teachers in these secondary schools were as good as or better than their counterparts at the universities. Most were gifted educators as well as scholars and encouraged creativity among their students. The schools were demanding and discriminating and did not admit or keep anyone unable to meet their standards. Graduating with high honors from one of these schools ensured admission to any university and an almost certain association with some of the top scientists of Europe. A good number of the most prominent Hungarian-American scientists went on to further their education at the great German universities, such as Berlin, Göttingen, Heidelberg, Freiburg, Tübingen, and Leipzig, which were the Harvards, Stanfords, Princetons, Yales, Cornells, and

MITs of their day. Having left Hungary because of the limited opportunities available in that small, dismembered country after World War I and then having fled Germany because of the rise of Hitler and nazism during the 1930s, most of them ultimately wound up in the United States at some of the top American universities and research institutes. The opportunity their adopted homeland provided for the émigrés was amply rewarded by the breadth of the scientists' discoveries.

Hollywood and the Hungarians

There is much to be said for the contention that the so-called American way of life, as portrayed by its most influential purveyors, the films of Hollywood, was to a large degree a creation of the Hungarian mind. This contention is based largely on the pioneering work of the Hungarian immigrants Adolph Zukor and William Fox, two of Hollywood's first film moguls. This view is also based on the heavy presence of Hungarians in the film capital after the establishment of the initial film studios there in 1911.

In Hollywood's halcyon days, Hungarian Americans constituted such a significant portion of the work

Hungarian-born film pioneer Adolph Zukor received a special Academy Award in 1948 in recognition of more than 40 years of service to the film industry. He served as the chairman of the board of Paramount Pictures from 1935 to 1966.

force at every level of the filmmaking process that some of the studios posted signs to the effect that "in this studio it is not enough to be a Hungarian." There were so many Hungarian screenwriters named "László"—a popular Hungarian first name—that an oft-told Tinseltown joke had it that in order to become successful in the field "it was not enough to be Hungarian . . . one [also] had to be called László."

Zukor and Fox were among the founders of the American film industry, yet when they went into the business of cinema, neither of them had more than an inkling of its real potential. But each possessed a shrewd understanding of the public's need for entertainment, a desire that they believed the fledgling film industry could fulfill.

Zukor was trained as an upholsterer and furrier in his native Hungary but after immigrating to the United States found work as a film salesman. The world of film fascinated him, and in 1913 he produced his first film, *The Count of Monte Cristo*, which had long been a perennial favorite on the stage. The presence in the title role of the matinee idol James O'Neill (himself an immigrant, from Ireland, and the father of one of the greatest playwrights, Eugene O'Neill), who had long been associated in the public's mind with the play, guaranteed Zukor a popular success. He went on to make the first American-produced full-length feature, *The Prisoner of Zenda*. After moving to California, Zukor founded Paramount Pictures and established Hollywood as the center of this new industry. He was soon followed by others, including fellow Hungarian William Fox, who established the Fox Film Corporation, the predecessor of 20th Century-Fox. Fox liked to boast that "no second of those contained in the twenty-four hours ever passed but that the name of William Fox was on the screen being exhibited in some theatre in some part of the world."

The art that Zukor, Fox, and other Hungarian-American cineasts brought to the silver screen entertained millions around the world. In the process, their own idealized view of life, drawn in part from their middle-class upbringing in Hungary, soon came to be equated with reality. Historian Emil Lengyel claims in his *Americans from Hungary* that the life "they repre-

The classical composer and pianist Béla Bartók, who immigrated to the United States in 1940, endeavored to create a genuinely Hungarian musical style and wanted to revitalize Hungarian musical life. Hungarian folk music provided the basis for much of his work.

sented as the American way of life, became *the* American way of life in the eyes of hundreds of millions from Murmansk to Capetown.''

Zukor and Fox were only two among many Hungarian Americans who helped create the legend of Hollywood. Many of the great directors of the day were Hungarian. These included George Cukor, noted for sophisticated comedies such as *Adam's Rib* and *The Philadelphia Story* as well as for *David Copperfield*, *Little Women*, and *A Star is Born*; Sir Alexander Korda (originally Sándor Kellner), a producer and director who aside from a successful stint in Hollywood is remembered as the savior of the British film industry; and Michael Curtiz (originally Mihály Kertész), the ''all-American'' director of such quintessential Hollywood pictures as *Angels with Dirty Faces*, *Casablanca*, *Yankee Doodle Dandy*, and *Mildred Pierce*. The tradition is carried on today by, among others, the talented young director and writer Jim Jarmusch, creator of the offbeat and critically acclaimed *Stranger than Paradise*, *Down by Law*, and *Mystery Train*. And there were and are hundreds of other famous Hungarian Americans in the film industry, from the much-beloved actor Leslie Howard, who started his life in Hungary as Arpád Steiner, through the beautiful Gabor sisters, Zsa Zsa, Eva, and Magda, to Tony Curtis (originally Bernard Schwartz). The best-known portrayer of Dracula, Bela Lugosi, began his career on the Budapest stage. And although not usually thought of as a film star, the great Harry Houdini, magician and escape artist extraordinaire, made several movies. He was born in Budapest as Ehrich Weiss.

The Arts

Although enormously talented, Hungarian-American artists generally had to work harder than their counterparts in the sciences to gain recognition. Béla Bartók, for example, one of the greatest 20th-century composers, immigrated to the United States in 1940. He died a bitterly disappointed man in New York City five years later, believing that his work had been neither understood nor appreciated by the American public. The famed architect Marcel Breuer, an advocate of the theories of the Bauhaus school, which emphasize functionalism and severity of line, faced similar initial difficulties in gaining understanding of his work.

These disappointments, however, were more than counterbalanced by the successes of others. Hungarian Americans have compiled a particularly notable record of success in the area of concert music. Since the 1930s, many of America's great symphony orchestras have been directed by expatriate Hungarians, all of whom received their training at the famed Liszt Academy of Music in Budapest. These have included Fritz Reiner

Hungarian-American architect Marcel Breuer studied and taught at the famous Bauhaus School of Design in Weimar, Germany. He immigrated to the United States in 1937 to teach architecture at Harvard. Breuer's bold architectual designs, among them the Whitney Museum of American Art in New York City, are distinguished by his skillful use of natural materials that blend with the surroundings.

of Pittsburgh, Chicago, and New York, George Széll of Cleveland, Eugene Ormandy of Philadelphia, Antal Doráti of Minneapolis and Washington, D.C., and Sir George Solti of Chicago. The work of these men was made easier by the talent of such gifted Hungarian instrumentalists as the violinist Joseph Szigeti and the cellist János Starker. The piano virtuoso André Watts is half Hungarian, having been born to a Hungarian mother and a black American father in Nuremberg, Germany. Jazz pianist Keith Jarrett also can claim some Hungarian ancestry.

Hungarian Americans have also produced their share of excellent visual artists. One of the first and the best known of these was the classical sculptor Alex-

Hungarian-American volleyball star Karch Kiraly smashes a powerful spike over the net at the Japan Cup for Men's Volleyball Tournament in Tokyo, 1986. Kiraly, who is regarded as one of the world's greatest volleyball players, led the United States to the gold medal in the 1988 Summer Olympics in Seoul, Korea.

Former professional football player and entertainer Joe Namath (front left) and Tim Browne, a participant at the Namath/Dockery Football Camp. Namath, who is of Hungarian descent, was a star quarterback for the New York Jets and was elected to the Pro Football Hall of Fame in 1985.

ander Finta, the Hungarian Rodin, whose works can be found in museums throughout the Western world. The wood engraver Joseph Domján is perhaps the best-known living Hungarian-American artist. Others include the graphic artist Lájos Szalay, the painter Stephen Juharos, the Byzantine icon painter Endre Fazekas, and the engraver Sándor Bodó. All graduated from the College of Fine Arts in Budapest before coming to the United States.

Sports

Evidence of the Hungarian Americans' success at assimilating into the mainstream has been their achievements in that most American of enthusiasms, big-time sports. At present, the most prominent Hungarian-American athlete is volleyball great Karch Kiraly, whose combination of quickness, grace, and power led the United States to the gold medal in the 1988 Summer Olympic Games at Seoul, Korea. Kiraly is generally regarded as the world's foremost volleyball player. His father, a prominent physician, left Hungary for the United States after the failed uprising of 1956.

Dancers perform at the Csardes Ball of the Hungarian Cultural Society in Château Lacombe, Canada, in 1971. Folk ensembles have helped preserve Hungarian traditions in North America.

HUNGARIAN AND AMERICAN

The United States and Canada have been good to the Hungarian immigrants. They offered the sons and daughters of this small but gifted nation hope and freedom from persecution and allowed them to advance according to the best of their abilities.

In turn, the immigrants and their ancestors have been good to their new homeland. Seeing it as a land of unlimited opportunity they brought to it a desire to work, a determination to succeed, knowledge, and intellectual and artistic abilities. While the lives of the newcomers were not always easy and many had to overcome poverty and prejudice, most endured, and most succeeded. A number of them did so beyond their wildest dreams and expectations, reaching plateaus of achievement that would have been unthinkable in their much-beloved but small homeland across the sea.

Most of the nearly 2 million men and women of the United States and Canada who claim Hungary as the land of their ancestors are average citizens who serve their new countries through their work and their dedication to family and nation. Among them are tens of thousands of highly gifted persons—most of them native born, but aware of their ancestry—who populate the upper levels of North American scientific, scholarly, economic, cultural, and artistic life. Although most Hungarian Americans are neither potential Nobel

103

The opening of the new Hungarian Heritage Center in New Brunswick, New Jersey, in 1985 served notice that Hungarian culture was flourishing in the United States. Hungarian-American artist Joseph Domján, whose wood engravings enhance the collections of many museums around the world, was on hand for the opening.

laureates nor future J. P. Morgans, they have contributed and will continue to contribute greatly to life in the United States and Canada. Like the members of other immigrant groups that have made their home on this continent, their drive, creativity, and attachment to the lands that offered them or their ancestors hope make them valued citizens without whom American society would be quite different indeed.

Although Hungarian Americans may no longer speak Hungarian at home, read Hungarian-language newspapers, live in predominantly Hungarian neighborhoods, or worship at Hungarian churches, most are aware of their roots, and many are actively involved in preserving and renewing their heritage.

There are manifold examples of such activity. These include the establishment or reestablishment of folk ensembles and other cultural groups in scores of North American cities; efforts to preserve the records of Hungarians in American and Canadian life through the establishment of libraries, archival collections, and museums; and intellectual exchanges both among Hungarian Americans themselves and with the intellectual leaders of Hungary.

The creation of folk ensembles has helped preserve Hungarian music and dance in North America. Folk ensembles of high artistic quality have been established in New York, Toronto, Chicago, San Francisco, Pittsburgh, Los Angeles, and elsewhere. They meet every year in national competitions called *pontozók*, which bring together scores of young Hungarians to celebrate the artistic achievements of their nation. Many of these ensembles also participate in such contests in Hungary, where they meet with other groups from all over the world.

One of the leading institutions in the effort to preserve the records of Hungarian Americans is the American Hungarian Foundation of New Brunswick, New Jersey. Its significant book, archival, and museum collections will soon move into the new Hungarian Heritage Center in the vicinity of Rutgers University, with which it is affiliated. Once relocated, the Hungarian Heritage Center, headed by its founder, the Reverend August J. Molnar, will undoubtedly become the most important depository of source materials on the history and achievements of Hungarians in North America.

Another important organization dedicated to the preservation of Hungarian-American history is the Rákóczi Foundation of Toronto, Canada, and Union, New Jersey. Named after the famous early-18th-century Hungarian patriot Prince Ferenc Rákóczi and founded in the mid-1970s by a former Hungarian Royal Army officer, Nicholas Korponay, the Rákóczi Foundation has sponsored numerous scholarly competitions and published many important books on Hungary and Hungarian achievements in the world. It also sponsors the *Hungarian Heritage Review*, edited by Paul Pulitzer, whose name is known to most Americans largely through the activities of his famous relative, Joseph Pulitzer.

Professor Jenö Bárdos lectures on Hungarian history at Rutgers University in New Jersey. Unless there is a new wave of immigration, Hungarian culture will prosper in North America only if each new generation of Hungarian Americans is made aware of its heritage.

Hungarian and Hungarian-American intellectuals also meet periodically, both on this continent and in Europe, to exchange ideas. In Hungary the most important such gatherings—the quadrennial Mother Tongue Conferences and various other specialized meetings for specific disciplines—are usually sponsored by the Hungarian World Federation in cooperation with one or more of the research institutes of the Hungarian Academy of Sciences. These conferences bring together individuals from dozens of countries who are concerned with the preservation of the Hungarian language and culture and with the furthering of Hungarian intellectual achievements.

In the United States, the most significant similar meetings are the annual conferences of the Hungarian Society of Friends (Magyar Baráti Közösség), which is known more commonly as the *Itt-Ott* group, after the name of its journal. Begun in the late 1960s as an informal gathering of concerned Hungarian intellectuals, this group has grown tremendously during the past two decades. Nowadays, its annual conferences draw hundreds of participants from Europe, Latin America, and Australia as well as North America and Hungary. Its deliberations are open, its tolerance for divergent views very broad and well advertised, and its level of intellectual achievement very high. Most of its members are also involved in ongoing dialogues with intellectual and political leaders in Hungary in the hope of advancing the cause of progressive social, political, and intellectual reforms in the land of their ancestors.

Each immigrant group has felt the conflict that arises as the result of the need to assimilate into a new society while preserving elements of the traditional culture. Few have resolved it so well as the Hungarian Americans. If their pride in their ancestry ensures that Hungarian culture will survive in North America, then the already considerable success of Hungarian Americans promises an even brighter future for their children and descendants.

FURTHER READING

Dreisziger, N. F., et al. *Struggle and Hope: The Hungarian-Canadian Experience*. Toronto: McClelland and Stewart, 1982.

Endrey, Eugene. *Beg, Borrow, and Squeal*. New York: Pageant Press, 1963.

Fermi, Laura. *Illustrious Immigrants: The Intellectual Migration from Europe, 1930–1941*. Chicago: University of Chicago Press, 1968.

Gracza, Rezsoe, and Margaret Young Gracza. *The Hungarians in America*. Minneapolis: Lerner Publications, 1969.

Kosa, John. *Land of Choice: The Hungarians in Canada*. Toronto: University of Toronto Press, 1957.

Lengyel, Emil. *Americans from Hungary*. Westport, CT: Greenwood Press, 1974.

Széplaki, Miklos. *The Hungarians in America, 1583–1974: A Chronology and Fact Book*. Dobbs Ferry, NY: Oceana Publications, 1975.

Várdy, Steven Béla. *The Hungarian Americans*. Boston: Twayne, 1985.

Vasváry, Edmund. *Lincoln's Hungarian Heroes: The Participation of Hungarians in the Civil War, 1861–1865*. Washington, DC: Hungarian Reformed Federation of America, 1939.

INDEX

PICTURE CREDITS

STEVEN BÉLA VÁRDY, a professor of history at Duquesne University and an adjunct professor of East European history at the University of Pittsburgh, has been a visiting scholar at the Hungarian Academy of Sciences and the University of Budapest. He received a Ph.D. from Indiana University and has also studied at John Carroll University, Case Western Reserve University, and the University of Vienna. He is the author of numerous books about Hungarians, including *Triumph in Adversity: Studies in Hungarian Civilization* and *History of the Hungarian Nation*.

DANIEL PATRICK MOYNIHAN is the senior United States senator from New York. He is also the only person in American history to serve in the cabinets or subcabinets of four successive presidents—Kennedy, Johnson, Nixon, and Ford. Formerly a professor of government at Harvard University, he has written and edited many books, including *Beyond the Melting Pot, Ethnicity: Theory and Experience* (both with Nathan Glazer), *Loyalties,* and *Family and Nation.*